Tithing Today

BY KEITH MOORE

TITHING TODAY

© 2022 Keith Moore

ISBN: 978-1-940403-10-6

BK322

Faith Life International, Inc.
6009 Business Boulevard
Sarasota, FL 34240
941-702-7390
www.flintl.org

Unless otherwise indicated, all Scripture quotations in this book are from the King James Version of the Bible.

Table of Contents

CHAPTER	TITLE	PAGE
1	After the Order of Melchizedek	1
2	The Things That Are God's	37
3	Honor and Blessing	79
	Confession of Tithing	145
	Tithing Addendum to a Marriage Ceremony	147
	Works Cited	149

Chapter 1: After the Order of Melchizedek

Hebrews 7:8 says, "And here men that die receive tithes; but there he receiveth them, of whom it is witnessed that he liveth."

I want to talk about tithing *today*. I believe I have a directive of the Lord, and I believe it to be very significant. A lot of folks need to make some corrections in their finances, and we don't need to wait. It's an answer to why some have struggled so much and come up short.

We need to make sure we get it right and that we're doing what He told us to do. If we get it right and honor Him, what's going to happen? He will honor us. It will affect us. It will impact us directly and immediately.

The verse says, "Here men that die receive tithes." He says that in the present tense. "There he receives them," present tense, "of whom it is witnessed that he lives." Is this tithing in the New Testament? Is Hebrews in the New Testament?

There are about three chapters here in the New Testament, in the Book of Hebrews, that are dealing with the subject of tithing. Now that is a lot of precious New Testament real estate to be given to something that's no longer applicable to us, as many would have us believe.

Back in Hebrews 6:13, it says, "For when God made promise to Abraham, because he could swear by no greater, he sware by himself." That tells you there's nobody else out there bigger than God, or as great as Him. Verse 14 continues, "Saying, Surely blessing I will bless thee, and multiplying I will multiply thee." Does that sound like increase—not just financially, but in every way? "Surely blessing I will bless thee, and multiplying I will multiply thee. And so, after he had patiently endured, he obtained the promise." (6:13-15) A lot of things don't happen by the end of the week. They don't happen by the end of the year or in three years or five years. You have to stay with it, long-term. You don't *try* it for a little while and then quit; you *do* it, and you do it until you obtain it.

One might say, "Well, I've been standing on that for *X* amount of time." Glory to God! You're closer to it now than you've ever been. Don't quit now!

Verse 16 continues, "For men verily swear by the greater: and an oath for confirmation is to them an end of all strife. Wherein God, willing more abundantly to shew unto the heirs of promise the immutability of his counsel, confirmed it by an oath: That by two immutable things, in which it was impossible for God to lie, we might have a strong consolation, who have fled for refuge to lay hold upon the hope set before us: Which hope we have as an anchor of the soul, both sure and stedfast, and which entereth into that within the veil; Whither the forerunner is for us entered, even Jesus, made an high priest for ever after the order of Melchisedec." (6:16-20) Would you agree that Jesus is currently, present tense, our High Priest? You don't get any more "New Testament" than this.

And we are told that He is a High Priest after the order of Melchizedek. He gives verse after verse about this, in chapter seven and on into chapter eight. Why does he bring this up? Because Jesus is not a Priest after the order of Aaron, which was the priesthood under the Mosaic Law. He is a Priest after the order of Melchizedek, of whom we're not given much detail. But the little bit of detail we *are* given about Melchizedek concerns tithing.

He continues in Hebrews 7:1. "For this Melchisedec, king of Salem, priest of the most high God, who met Abraham returning from the slaughter of the kings, and blessed him." What did we just read about Abraham? God made a promise to him. What did He say back in 6:14? "Surely blessing I will bless thee." Is there a lot said in the Bible about blessing? To many people in modern times, it doesn't mean a thing. It is what they say after somebody sneezes: "Bless you." What does that mean to them? Not a thing. But to God, blessing *means* something. It's real. It is a release of power. When God says, "I bless you: increase, multiply, prosper, and succeed," in that word is empowerment.

It's like when Jesus told Peter, "Come." He couldn't do it until He told him. When Jesus told him to come to Him on the water, there was power in the word to give him faith to step out and power to cause it to come to pass. No word from God is void of power, so God's word of blessing is empowerment and enablement to prosper, to increase, and to succeed. If you are blessed in doing a thing, you are not doing it on your own, in your own strength. You have divine enablement, and you need to acknowledge it on a regular basis. When something goes so super and so great, and you are at the right place at the right time, and it just comes together, and people ask, "Man, how did you do that? *You* are good!" you say, "No, I had help. The Lord blessed me." You say, "He blessed me in it, and the blessing brought me favor, and the blessing brought me strength, and the blessing helped me to increase and get it done and succeed."

Are you interested in the blessing and in the empowerment and enablement of the Lord? Well, the priesthood is involved in the blessing, and it's in response to people honoring God.

Melchizedek was priest of the Most High God. Now we have to remember this was a long time before the Law. This was in ancient times. There's no Moses, there's no Ten Commandments, there's no Old Testament, there's no Bible at all. Abraham's time is an ancient time compared to ours. But there was a priest of the Most High God long before Aaron ever lived, and long before the priests or the Levites—none of that existed. It came much, much later. So then, how did they have a priest? Where did he come from? How did he know he was a priest? And here's a big question: How did Abraham know how to tithe? Where did he get it? And why did he do it?

You hear a lot of people say, "Tithing is under the Law," and that shows their ignorance of the Scriptures. Tithing was long, long before the Law.

Abraham is the father of faith. Not only did he tithe before tithing existed in any organized fashion, but he had faith. Before the Law, he lived by faith. Before the coming of Jesus, there were no faith seminars to attend. There were no Word churches or Word schools. How did Abraham learn how to have faith? How did he learn how to do that? He had a personal relationship with God. He got it personally from God, Who also taught him to tithe. It was pre-Law, pre-prophets, pre-everything. If tithing precedes the Law, then like walking by faith, tithing succeeds the Law.

Look again at Hebrews 7:1. "For this Melchisedec, king of Salem, priest of the most high God, who met Abraham returning from the slaughter of the kings, and blessed him." This is very significant. What was Melchizedek's role in this? You really only see two basic things that Melchizedek did. I'm sure he did more, but we have a record of the two things that he did: He received tithes, and he blessed Abraham. This is a forerunner of our High Priest.

We have a High Priest, our current, present High Priest, after the order of Melchizedek. I wonder how many people you would get to agree and say, "Our High Priest blesses us today." Well, why remove the tithing part? Why take that out? If He's after the order of Melchizedek, and tithing is done away with, that messes up the type, because that's part of the thing that Melchizedek did. He received the tithes, and he blessed Abraham.

Say this out loud: **He received tithes and blessed.**

That's what Melchizedek did, and Jesus, our High Priest, is a Priest like Melchizedek. So are we going to say that He is a Priest like Melchizedek, but that He doesn't do what Melchizedek did? That it's done away with? That's what people are saying.

Keep reading verse 2. "To whom also Abraham gave a tenth *part* of all." Did he tithe? He gave the tenth to Melchizedek. "…first being by interpretation King of righteousness, and after that also King of Salem, which is, King of peace; Without father, without mother, without descent, having neither beginning of days, nor end of life; but made like unto the Son of God;

abideth a priest continually." We have no record of his lineage, and he certainly had nothing to do with Aaron, because that was long before Aaron came on the scene. "Now consider how great this man was, unto whom even the patriarch Abraham gave the tenth of the spoils." (vv. 2-4) Was Abraham a tither? Yes, he was. His son was a tither; he got that from his father. But where did Abraham get it? He didn't get it from the Law, because the Law didn't exist. There were no Ten Commandments.

We have to get this straight. People say, "Tithing is under the Law." Again, that shows ignorance. Tithing predates the Law. Just like Abraham, having faith predates the Law. And you have to watch about saying tithing is no more, because then what do you say about faith? Are you going to say Abraham is not an example to us? Folks like to pick and choose. "Oh yes, I'm of the seed of Abraham, but I don't tithe. That has passed away." Really? Then you're not walking in the steps of Abraham as much as you thought.

Abraham believed God long before the revelation that the just shall walk by faith. He got it from God personally. It was a revelation of what was to come, past the Law. He also tithed long before there was any Law or Commandments, and he did it because he got it from God—the same place he got his faith. He got it from God. And he didn't do it to be justified in the eyes of the Lord. He did it out of honor, and the response was for God to bless him through his high priest. To Abraham, tithing wasn't a regulation, it was a revelation.

Many modern Christians tell us it has been done away with—that it isn't for us nowadays. Honoring God is not for us nowadays. Having a Priest after the order of Melchizedek is not for us nowadays— although it's all in the Book of Hebrews in the New Testament. They say that being blessed by your High Priest is not for us nowadays. No, that's a disconnect from some of the greatest truths in the Word. Do you know that most of the church world does not tithe? It's just a fact. Most of the church world does not tithe, and people have all kinds of reasons for it. One of the biggest ones is what we're talking about right now. People say, "That's just Old Testament." Then they usually say, "Old Testament. That's under the Law. That's not for us nowadays." And there's some dishonesty to that, because the truth is, a lot of folks don't care. They're not going to do it no matter what. They don't care how many scriptures you show them; they're not going to do it. It's not about scriptures; it's about looking for justification for what they're *not* doing, so there's dishonesty to it.

We're not about any condemnation, but do you want to know the truth? What will the truth do for you? It will make you free. We're tithers around here. My wife Phyllis and I are tithers personally, and Faith Life

After the Order of Melchizedek

Church Branson is a tithing church. Faith Life Church Sarasota is a tithing church. Moore Life Ministries is a tithing ministry. A lot of folks in the church are tithers, and I know a lot of folks are not. You might ask, "How do you know?" I just know it in my spirit. I purposely don't look at the giving records. I don't know personally what anyone gives, and I don't want to know. I know the total giving at the end of the quarters and end of the year, and that kind of thing, but it's not my business to try to keep up with individuals.

But I do know this: If you honor God, He will honor you. And I care about you. I don't want you to struggle financially. I want you to have the blessing of the tither, and I want you to have the protection of the tither. Didn't Malachi say that the Lord would rebuke the devourer for your sake? And when you say, "I don't believe in tithing. That's not for us. That's passed away," well then, the blessing is not for you, and the protection is not for you either, right?

I'm not trying to talk you into anything. You don't need to try to comply with what I think. You need to get it for yourself in the Bible. That's why we're reading scripture verses. Just open your heart to the scriptures. This is *not* about us tithing to churches. It's about us tithing to God. There is a big difference.

Hebrews 7:4 says, "Now consider how great this man was, unto whom even the patriarch Abraham gave the tenth of the spoils." (I want to remind you that we are reading about tithing in the New Testament.) "And verily they that are of the sons of Levi, who receive the office of the priesthood, have a commandment to take tithes of the people according to the law, that is, of their brethren, though they come out of the loins of Abraham: But he whose descent is not counted from them received tithes of Abraham, and blessed him that had the promises." (vv. 4-6)

Say this out loud again: **He received tithes and blessed him.**

That's what Melchizedek the high priest of God did: He received tithes, and He blessed him.

Verse 7 continues, "And without all contradiction the less is blessed of the better," the greater. "And here men that die receive tithes; but there he receiveth them, of whom it is witnessed that he liveth." (vv. 7-8) Do we have a High Priest today? What kind of High Priest is He? He's not a High Priest after the order of Aaron, right? We're not justified by keeping the Law. And we're not justified and clean by the offering of the blood of animals through the Aaronic priesthood—which is why Jesus is not a High Priest after the order of Aaron. But He *is* a High Priest like somebody else was:

Melchizedek, who was the high priest of God long before Aaron and Moses.

"And here men that die receive tithes." Is that past tense or present tense? "But there he receiveth them, of whom it is witnessed that he liveth." Is Jesus alive today? Do we have a High Priest right now? What kind of High Priest is He? He is like Melchizedek. Well, what did Melchizedek do? You can imagine some things, but from the Scriptures, the only thing we really know is that he received tithes, and he blessed him.

"And as I may so say, Levi also, who receiveth tithes, payed tithes in Abraham. For he was yet in the loins of his father, when Melchisedec met him." (vv. 9-10)

"If therefore perfection were by the Levitical priesthood, (for under it the people received the law,) what further need was there that another priest should rise after the order of Melchisedec, and not be called after the order of Aaron? For the priesthood being changed, there is made of necessity a change also of the law." (vv. 11-12) The priesthood changed; tithing didn't. Tithing hasn't changed.

"For he of whom these things are spoken pertaineth to another tribe, of which no man gave attendance at the altar. For it is evident that our Lord sprang out of Juda; of which tribe Moses spake nothing concerning priesthood. And it is yet far more evident: for that after the similitude of Melchisedec there ariseth another priest, Who is made, not after the law of a carnal commandment, but after the power of an endless life. For he testifieth, Thou art a priest for ever," in a specific way, "after the order of Melchisedec." (vv. 13-17) The only record of what he did was he received tithes, and he blessed Abraham.

Now is our High Priest, Jesus, a different priest from Melchizedek? That's what people are saying. Or is He the same kind of priest and doing the same kind of things, after the order of Melchizedek? "For there is verily a disannulling of the commandment going before for the weakness and unprofitableness thereof. For the law made nothing perfect, but the bringing in of a better hope did; by the which we draw nigh unto God. And inasmuch as not without an oath he was made priest: (For those priests were made without an oath; but this with an oath by him that said unto him," this is talking about Jesus, "The Lord sware and will not repent, Thou art a priest for ever after the order of Melchisedec.)" (vv. 18-21) Is this significant? We've heard it repeatedly.

Jesus is a Priest, *the* Priest, the High Priest of God, forever. And He's a Priest like Melchizedek was, after the order of Melchizedek.

"By so much was Jesus made a surety of a better testament. And they truly were many priests, because they were not suffered to continue by reason of death." They kept changing out the priests every generation because they died. "But this man," talking about Jesus, "because he continueth ever, hath an unchangeable priesthood." (vv. 22-24) His unchangeable Priesthood is after the order of Melchizedek.

Now the Aaronic priesthood was changed, but the type of priesthood Jesus is to us today was foreshadowed by Melchizedek.

"Wherefore he is able also to save them to the uttermost that come unto God by him, seeing he ever liveth to make intercession for them. For such <u>an</u> high priest became us, who is holy, harmless, undefiled, separate from sinners, and made higher than the heavens; Who needeth not daily, as those high priests, to offer up sacrifice, first for his own sins, and then for the people's: for this he did once, when he offered up himself. For the law maketh men high priests which have infirmity; but the word of the oath, which was since the law, maketh the Son, who is consecrated for evermore." (vv. 25-28)

Say this out loud: **I have a High Priest after the order of Melchizedek.**

Are we the children of Abraham? If you read through Romans 4 and Galatians 3 in detail, you will see that those passages tell us we are the children of Abraham. And just like he had faith and was justified for his faith, we have faith and are justified by our faith. Abraham learned from God long before Moses and the Ten Commandments and the Law. Do you know what else Abraham learned long before the Law? He learned how to give the tenth of it all to the high priest, and he learned how to receive the blessing when he did. He was blessed. He had silver and gold, and so many employees, camels, donkeys, and sheep that the land couldn't hold them. This is the exact same blessing described in Malachi 3:10. It states there that when we tithe and honor Him, He will open the windows of heaven and pour out until there's not enough room to receive it. And right in the middle of this passage on tithing is where the Lord says, "For I am the Lord, I change not…" And yet, many are saying He's changed and doesn't care about such things anymore.

Not only did Abraham have all of that, but he also received the desire of his heart. When it seemed impossible for he and Sarah to have a child, they had one. They had to stand and believe God, but they had a son. And God is bringing it to pass today that Abraham's seed is like the sand on the seashore and like the stars in the sky. We are part of that group!

Abraham's seed ought to act like Abraham: They ought to believe like Abraham, they ought to obey like Abraham, they ought to honor God like Abraham, and they ought to tithe like Abraham.

I know a lot of people will fuss with this, and they will find reasons not to do it, but like I said, some of these people are just dishonest. It wouldn't make a difference how clear it is in the Word, they're not going to do it. So it's not about the Word. To them, it's about money.

I am saying this again: This is *not* about you tithing to our churches or ministries or any other group. This is about you and me tithing to God. The text said "… And he gave **HIM** tithes of all." (Genesis 14:20) Abraham didn't just give it to some group or institution; he gave the tithes to **HIM**.

It's about bringing our tithe to our High Priest, and Him receiving our tithes. And then it's about Him empowering us and enabling us to increase and succeed and prosper—because we are blessed. "The blessing of the Lord, it maketh rich, and He addeth no sorrow with it." (Proverbs 10:22) If I wasn't a tither already, I would be changing right now.

In Genesis 14, we have the only scriptures about Melchizedek that I've found. If you just get this one thing settled in you, it would be huge: I have a great High Priest, passed into the heavens, Jesus, the Son of God. He's there between me and the Father. He represents the Father to me, and He represents me to the Father, and He ever lives to make intercession. That's not talking about prayer; *intercession* is a legal term. Another word that is used in the Scriptures is "Mediator." Jesus represents us at the throne.

Say this out loud: **I have representation at the throne of God. I have an Advocate, Jesus Christ the Righteous.**

When we do the things we're supposed to do, our High Priest has authority from the throne to bless us. It's no small thing to have His enablement and empowerment in our life and on our life down here, day-to-day, as we live, and as we come and go. We desperately need it, and with it, the things that were so difficult become easy, and the things that were impossible become possible. With enough grace, and with enough help, and with enough blessing, you can achieve anything. You can receive anything. It doesn't get too big. But we need His help. We need His blessing. Would you admit that you need His help? You know you need His blessing. You're not enough on your own. You know you need it.

Genesis 14 starts out telling about how the kings got into a war. There were multiple kings, and multiple armies, and basically the whole country was engulfed in war. This was where Abraham was living, and where his nephew Lot and his family were living. Lot's family had moved to Sodom, and there was war all over the country.

In verse 8, it tells about how they came and joined the battle and had war. In verse 10, the kings of Sodom and Gomorrah fled and fell there, so they were defeated. Then verse

11 says, "And they took all the goods of Sodom and Gomorrah, and all their victuals, and went their way." Sodom and Gomorrah were great cities of the day. It would be like some of the greatest cities in our country today. They were highly populated, and they were advanced and civilized for their time.

"And they took Lot, Abram's brother's son, who dwelt in Sodom, and his goods, and departed." (v. 12) Do you think Lot shouldn't have been living there? When you go where you're not supposed to be, bad things can happen. (See Genesis 13.) Was it the will of God for Lot and his family and all their possessions to be taken? No. But when you get out of the will of God, you get out from under the protection of God, bad things can happen to you. God is not doing it to you; you're just in a place out of His will, where you're not protected.

Do you want to live under the protective shadow of the Almighty? Then you need to make sure you are where you're supposed to be. You need to go where you're sent and stay where you're stationed. Stay in your place, because that's a safe place, a protected place, and a prosperous place.

You cannot just measure prosperity in dollar bills. People say, "Well, I'm only making so much money." Yes, but how much are you not *losing*? Besides that, who said you couldn't make more money where you are? So many times people are not thinking correctly.

We received a testimony from some folks who said they jumped up and moved to the other side of the country for a more glamorous, higher-paying job, and they left their place in a good church. They told about how everything went bad. Why? They were out of their place. And that glamorous job turned into nothing. Then they had all sorts of other expenses and problems.

After the Order of Melchizedek

Being in the right place is where your protection and prosperity are, and a lot of your prosperity is in what you *don't* have to spend: the sicknesses you don't have, the lawsuits you don't have, and the divorces you don't have. You don't have expenses from the accidents that you *don't* have. And it goes on and on and on. A lot of us don't know how prosperous we are. There's so much we *didn't* have to spend and pay and go through in the past year or two or five or ten, because when you are where you're supposed to be, you are protected. That's a big part of your prosperity.

The Bible says they took Lot (his brother's son) and all his goods, and they left. Usually that would've been the end of it. Lot and his family were never going to see their possessions again, and they were never going to see each other again. They would have been split up and sold as slaves, and the people would have pocketed the money; that would've been the end of it. That's what happened 999 times out of

1000. But Lot had some relatives, and one in particular who knew God. He knew how to believe God, and he was a tither: Uncle Abram. Uncle Abe.

This was war. I don't know if they were in chains, or if they were separated, or if they had witnessed horror, abuse, and killing, but don't you think when they saw Uncle Abram coming, they were happy? Never in their life were they so glad to see Uncle Abram. I don't know what kind of conversation they had when they had parted, but it's obvious they felt like they didn't need Uncle Abram anymore—they had moved to Sodom. But it turns out they *did* need him.

Keep reading in Genesis. Verse 14 says, "And when Abram heard that his brother was taken captive, he armed his trained servants, born in his own house, three hundred and eighteen,… And he divided himself against them, he and his servants, by night, and smote them, and pursued them unto Hobah, which is on the left hand of Damascus. And he brought back all the goods, and also brought again his brother Lot, and his goods, and the women also, and the people." (vv. 14-16) They didn't lose a single one. They didn't lose a wife, they didn't lose a child, and they didn't lose a cow or a sheep. They got all their gold back. They got all their furniture back, and their vases and shoes and socks. It said they got it *all* back—*all* the goods. They got their hot sauce and their tomatoes and stuff they had put up. They got it all.

Verse 17 continues, "And the king of Sodom went out to meet him after his return from the slaughter of Chedorlaomer, and of the kings that were with him, at the valley of Shaveh, which is the king's dale." And Abram ignored them and went to Melchizedek. You know, you need to know what comes first. The king of Sodom was supposed to be the "bigwig" around there. He wasn't just the president, he was the king. But the truth is, he had been crushed

After the Order of Melchizedek

and defeated. Their treasury was stripped, their people were taken, and at that present moment, the king of Sodom was king over nothing. The people were not there, the gold was not there, the stuff was not there… until guess who comes up with all of it trailing behind him? Abraham. Abraham could have made *himself* king of Sodom and Gomorrah on the spot. He's got it all: the power, the soldiers, the stuff. He could have said, "Well, I'm king now. I went and took it, I have it, it's mine." Which is why the king of Sodom—instead of sending for Abraham—went to meet him. He needs to talk to this Abraham. He's scared of what's going to happen next.

Abraham sees the king approaching, with what little entourage he could scrape up, and his crown and things. He tells the king, "Yeah, I'll talk to you in a minute…" He must have, because we see in the next verse that Melchizedek had come. "And Melchizedek king of Salem brought forth bread and wine: and he was the priest of the most high God." (v. 18) Hallelujah! Do we know a Priest? We know the Priest of the Most High God. And is He not the same kind of Priest as Melchizedek? When the New Testament gives two or three chapters to the subject, you ought to pay attention to it.

Verse 19 continues, "And he blessed him…" He's a blessing priest. "And he blessed him, and said, Blessed be Abram of the most high God, possessor of heaven and earth: And blessed be the most high God, which hath delivered thine enemies into thy hand." And what happened? Is Abraham tithing because it's the Law? Is he tithing to justify himself in the eyes of God? This has got nothing to do with the Law or commandments. What is he doing? He is honoring the God Who just saved his life. He is honoring God, Who spared his kin folks. He got Lot, he got his wife, he got his girls, he got the sons-in-law, he got the possessions, everything. And when the high priest came and said, "And blessed be the most high God, which hath delivered thine enemies into thy hand," Abraham said, *"That's exactly right. The reason I'm standing here breathing is because the Almighty God was with me and kept me. There's no way we could have done that without God's help."* And he tithed. His response was tithing. (vv. 19-20) He's saying he wouldn't have any of it except God enabled him to get it, and get it back, so he gave the tenth. There was no Malachi 3. There were no Gospels. There was no Romans or Galatians. There was none of that. But understand, honoring God and thanking God has always been right—and it will always be right.

Some ask, "Do I have to tithe?" Obviously you do not. Most of the world does not. It's not about *having* to tithe. It's not about keeping a rule. It's not about a law. It's about honoring God, and you'll find throughout the Scriptures that honor and blessing go together. When you honor Him, He is going to honor you. And the way He

After the Order of Melchizedek

honors you is by blessing you, and that blessing makes rich, and that blessing protects.

"And he gave him tithes of all. And the king of Sodom said unto Abram, Give me the persons, and take the goods to thyself." He's willing for him to take all the money, as long as he can have somebody to be king over. "And Abram said to the king of Sodom, I have lift up mine hand unto the Lord, the most high God, the possessor of heaven and earth." Does Abraham know Who his Source is? Does he know Who his God is? He said, "I will not take from a thread even to a shoelatchet, and that I will not take any thing that is thine, lest thou shouldest say, I have made Abram rich." (vv. 20-23) He's saying, *Nobody is ever going to be able to say that anybody is my Source except God. That's why I tithe. I know Who my Source is.*

What kind of priest was Melchizedek? He was not an Aaronic priest, not connected to the Law at all. Melchizedek was a priest of the Most High God who came and spoke blessing over Abraham, who then responded by tithing.

Say this out loud: **Tithing and blessing. Blessing and tithing. Tithing and blessing.**

When God takes care of you, what do you do? Do you tithe? When He protects you, what do you do? Give thanks, show honor, and tithe? Then what happens? You get blessed. Then? You tithe. Then you get blessed. Then you tithe, right? Honor and blessing. Tithing is honoring God. Blessing is honoring you. Can you see this?

Now don't misunderstand this. We cannot buy the blessing. We cannot buy protection, or a healing or a salvation. The value of these things is far beyond our ability to earn or purchase. But honoring is not buying. Abraham gave tithes **<u>AFTER</u>** he was delivered and prospered. Tithing and giving offerings freely, willingly, and gladly is the response of a thankful heart to a faithful God.

If you have it in your heart to do it, pray this out loud:

Father God, I acknowledge that You are my Source. You are the Creator of the heavens and the earth. You are my Protector. You are my Provider. So I gladly honor You with the holy portion. I'm a tither. I present my tithe to the High Priest, and I receive the blessing. Hallelujah. In Jesus' Name. Amen.

Chapter 2: The Things That Are God's

I believe I have a directive of the Lord that we need to examine ourselves in this area, and we need to make any adjustments that should be made, because God wants to bless us. If we don't get this right, it will limit us and our abilities to help others. There's a lot of wrong thinking on the subject of tithing, and a lot of misconceptions and ignorance. We don't want to be ignorant or confused.

Hebrews 7:8 says, "And here men that die receive tithes; but there he receiveth them, of whom it is witnessed that he liveth." Hallelujah! He lives!

We saw in chapter 1 that Jesus is our High Priest. Seven times in the Book of Hebrews, just in a couple of chapters, we are told that Jesus is a great High Priest after the order of Melchizedek. Not too much is told about Melchizedek, but what we do see is that

Melchizedek met Abraham when he returned from victory over the enemy kings. That was when he got Lot back, and his kin folks and all their possessions, and the city and all their possessions. Melchizedek, who was king of righteousness and king of Salem, or "peace," and also priest of the Most High God, met Abraham, and he blessed him, and they were acknowledging the blessing of the Lord.

Now, keeping it in context, what are they talking about? Well, there's no way, naturally speaking, Abraham and his handful of trained servants and friends should have been able to defeat those armies. There's no way that should have happened. And not only did they win, they got all their kin folks back. They got all of their possessions back, everything. So they are blessing God and acknowledging that they are blessed. When the high priest Melchizedek talked about the blessing of the Lord being on him, the Bible says Abraham responded and gave him tithes of all. Now that was a substantial amount of money and things, because it was the money and all the wealth of the city that they had recaptured. So this was a sizable amount of money. *Tithe* means "tenth," or we would say today "ten percent."

So Abraham gave Melchizedek ten percent of everything, of all, and Melchizedek blessed Abraham.

A lot of people, churchgoing people, will tell you that tithing is just in the Old Testament, and that tithing was part of the Law and under the Law. They say it's not for us nowadays, and it is passed away. But you have to watch about that. That's the same thing that a lot of people are saying about healing—that it's not for us today. Healing and miracles are not for us nowadays, that it's passed away. That's the same thing a whole lot of people are also saying about speaking in tongues. "Oh, that's not for us. It's all passed away." You

The Things That Are God's

have to watch about "it's passed away…." God doesn't change. He does not change.

There also needs to be some mind renewal. It has become popular among some circles to speak disparagingly about the Law. You can hear it in the tone of people's voices. They say, "Oh, that's just the Law," and they use a disrespectful tone in their voice.

However, the *New* Testament, says, "Wherefore the **law is holy**, and the commandment **holy**, and **just**, and **good."** (Romans 7:12) This doesn't say the Law used to be, or *was good,* but that it *IS* good. "For we know that **the law is spiritual**: but I am carnal, sold under sin." (v. 14)

Is there a present-day use for the Law? Yes, there is.

"But we know that **the law is good**, if a man use it lawfully." (1 Timothy 1:8)

"I agree that the Law is excellent—provided it is legitimately used…" (Goodspeed)

"Now we know that the Law is good, if a man uses it in the way it should be used…" (Weymouth)

"Do we then make void the law through faith? God forbid: yea, **we establish the law**." (Romans 3:31)

Just because something is in the Law, statutes, and ordinances given by Moses, that doesn't mean it's old or obsolete.

We are not redeemed from the Law, but rather from the Curse of the Law.

The Holy Spirit through the writers of the New Testament continually refer to the "scriptures" in what we call the Old Testament. Why continually refer to something hundreds of times that isn't even applicable to us anymore?

The Things That Are God's

The truth is, right is still right. Good is still good. Holy is still holy.

Not worshipping false gods, not murdering, not stealing, honoring God and father and mother, these and everything He has revealed is just as right, good, and holy as it ever was. To slight any part of the Word of God and to tell others they should mostly ignore it is a grave mistake.

"Let your light so shine before men, that they may see your good works, and glorify your Father which is in heaven. Think not that I am come to destroy the law, or the prophets: I am not come to destroy, but to fulfil. For verily I say unto you, Till heaven and earth pass, one jot or one tittle shall in no wise pass from the law, till all be fulfilled. Whosoever therefore shall break one of these least commandments, and shall teach men so, he shall be called the least in the kingdom of heaven: but whosoever shall do and teach them, the same shall be called great in the kingdom of heaven." (Matthew 5:16-19)

Has heaven and earth passed away? Have all the prophecies in the Bible been fulfilled? No, they have not. So those who are despising and belittling the Law and the prophets are making a big mistake.

All that God has ever spoken was, is, and will always be true, right, and good. Heaven and earth will pass away, but His words, **<u>all of them</u>**, will never pass away.

What has changed is that Jesus's blood and sacrifice has redeemed us once and for all. Therefore, no other animal blood sacrifices are to be offered. And because He became sin and gave us His righteousness, we are not saved or made righteous by doing or being good or by keeping the Law. We are saved by faith in Him alone.

"For by grace are ye saved through faith; and that not of yourselves: it is the gift of

God: Not of works, lest any man should boast." (Ephesians 2:8-9)

After the resurrection of our Lord and the pouring out of the Holy Spirit in Acts 2, when the leaders came together in council, their consensus was that it was not necessary for the new believers among the Gentiles to keep the Law in order to be saved. However, they reminded them that the Law was being read every Sabbath Day, implying that they needed to and should continue hearing it.

"For Moses of old time hath in every city them that preach him, being read in the synagogues every sabbath day." (Acts 15:21)

Observing and implementing the unchanging truths of God's statutes in our daily life is not the same as trying to keep them in order to be saved.

Say this out loud: **The Law is holy. The Law is right. The Law is good. God does not change.**

Abraham was long before the Law. I went into this in a lot of detail in chapter 1. Long before there was the mount where the fire came down, and long before God gave them the tablets in stone with the Ten Commandments and all the statutes and the ordinances that went with them—the Law—a long time before any of that happened, Abraham gave tithes of all to Melchizedek.

So where did Abraham learn how to tithe? There was no Bible, there were no Ten Commandments, there was no Law, and there was no Moses. So why was he tithing? Where did he get this? He learned it the same place he learned how to have faith in God. Abraham walked by faith and is held up as an example of faith to you and me in the New Testament, in the Book of Romans and in the Book of Galatians. He is called "the father of all them that believe." And we are to "walk in the steps of that faith of our father Abraham." (Romans 4:11-12) Aren't we who are in Christ called "his children, the seed of Abraham"?

He was made right because of his faith, pointing to the day when that would be available to all, salvation and righteousness by faith and grace in Jesus. Well, he also tithed long before any Law. So if his walking by faith is right for us today, why wouldn't his tithing be right for us? Why would that be different?

There are many folks who just haven't studied the Word on this. They've heard some of the things that are contrary to Scripture, and they just don't know. When they are enlightened, they'll make changes.

We're talking about you and me tithing to God. And as we get further into this, talking about where the tithe should go, we'll see that's where being led by the Spirit comes

The Things That Are God's

in. In the New Covenant, everybody is supposed to know God for themselves and not just follow legalities and rituals and rules. But we've got to get this settled first.

What is tithing about? Abraham wasn't trying to be justified in the eyes of God by his tithing. He wasn't trying to keep a law or a rule—because there was no law or rule. So why did he tithe? He got it from God by revelation, just like he got living by faith by revelation, and it pointed to the future, to the day you and I are living. The reason he tithed was to honor God. He's honoring God, saying, "I wouldn't be alive right now. No way would we have won these battles. No way would we all be safe and come back here. No way would we have saved everybody and gotten everybody's life back. Plus we also got all this stuff! We got all the money! We got all the things!" He's acknowledging, "God kept us, God protected us, God provided for us, and the reason we got all this increase was because of God. So here, Lord, is the tenth portion," and he honored God. He can't send it to God in heaven. God doesn't need it in heaven. So he gave it to God's high priest, and then the high priest was now authorized and anointed of God to turn around and bless Abraham. What is tithing about? It's about honor and blessing.

Has honor been done away with in this New Covenant? Has Blessing been done away with? Are you still interested in honoring God? Well, should we honor God with more than our words? Should we honor Him with our deeds, our actions, and our possessions? Should we still acknowledge that we wouldn't have anything if it wasn't for God? And when a deal goes through, and we're able to work a week, and we get paid, and some success brings increase, should we acknowledge that if God hadn't helped us, there's no way we would have gotten it done? Well, the correct response is to tithe, and when you tithe and honor God, He blesses you.

Say this out loud: **Honor and blessing. I honor Him; He blesses me.**

That's how it has always worked. It worked that way before the Law, and it works that way after the Law. I expect it will still work that way a million years from now.

The Lord said it's Him that gives us power to get wealth. (Deuteronomy 8:18) We should acknowledge that. And He said, "Those that honour me, I will honour." (1 Samuel 2:30)

In Matthew 22:15, it says, "Then went the Pharisees, and took counsel how they might entangle him [Jesus] in his talk. And they sent out unto him their disciples with the Herodians, saying, Master, we know that thou art true, and teachest the way of God in truth, neither carest thou for any man: for thou regardest not the person of men." You don't play any favorites. They're trying to set Him up. "Tell us therefore, What thinkest thou? Is it lawful to give tribute

The Things That Are God's

unto Caesar, or not? But Jesus perceived their wickedness, and said, Why tempt ye me, ye hypocrites?" (vv. 15-18) They're not genuinely trying to get an answer to this question. They want Him to say something they can use to get Him in trouble with the government, by talking about not paying taxes.

Jesus said, "Shew me the tribute money. And they brought unto him a penny." (v. 19) That wouldn't be like our penny. It would be more like a day's wages. "And he saith unto them, Whose is this image and superscription?" (v. 20) Whose picture is this, and what is written on it?

Now if I asked you to pull out some money right now, say a twenty-dollar bill, there's a picture on that twenty-dollar bill. Whose picture is that? It's Andrew Jackson, and it says, "Federal Reserve Note." And in another place it says, "United States of America." So we have pictures and writing on our money, too, don't we?

The Things That Are God's

Jesus asked them, "Whose picture is that and whose superscription?" Verse 21 continues, "They say unto him, Caesar's. Then saith he unto them, Render therefore unto Caesar the things which are Caesar's; and unto God the things that are God's." If it has his picture and name on it, it must be his. So give it to him.

Verse 21 in The Living Bible says, "Give it to Caesar if it is his, and give God everything that belongs to God."

The Message says, "Then give Caesar what is his, and give God what is his."

So according to Jesus, there were things that are Caesar's and should be given to Caesar, but there are also things that are God's that should be given to God.

Now what is considered God's? A lot of times you ask that question, and people will say, "Everything." But that's not right. Apparently Jesus didn't think that was right, because if all of it is God's, then you

The Things That Are God's

don't give any of it to Caesar. He said some of it was Caesar's. So we have to watch about religious thinking. It sounds good and seems good, but that doesn't make it true.

A lot of times you hear people say the same thing personally. "Well, everything I have is the Lord's." That's not true—and I can tell they don't believe it, because they're spending it on themselves. If it's all His, why are you spending it on you? And if it is all His, you could never give Him anything. You could never give Him an offering. Offerings couldn't exist, because anything you gave Him would just be returning what is His.

We need mind renewal in these areas. Jesus revealed that this tribute, this tax that Caesar's government—the Roman government—said the people owed them was Caesar's. He didn't say it wasn't fair, or that it was a waste of money. He didn't tell them to fight it. What did He say?

The Things That Are God's

"Give to them what is theirs, and give to God what is His."

Does the Internal Revenue Service (IRS) think that part of the money you receive is theirs? Are they confused or undecided about whether any of that money is theirs or not? No, and they don't stop at ten percent. So if they say, "That is our money. This "x" percent of what you earned is ours," according to the Bible, what should you say? You should say, "Okay. Here it is."

Some might say, "That's not right. I don't like that." It *is* right. Is your picture on that money? Is your name on that money? Well, then in one sense, it's not your money. You didn't print it. You're not the Federal Reserve. It's theirs, and if they say you owe it to them, then you do. Give them their money, with their name on it.

Some folks say, "Yeah, it just makes me so mad. It makes me so sick. They just waste so much money. They just blow it by the

The Things That Are God's

hundreds of millions and billions for nothing."

This is the way I look at it: There are always going to be people who just don't care anymore, and that just cuss and fuss about it. I'm going to say that it's *their* taxes that is being wasted. And my money, my taxes, are going to *good* things. It's going to keep a good strong military to keep us safe. It's going to a good infrastructure. It's going to keep us free and to keep us strong. That's where my money is going. All that money that they're blowing is from the folks that fuss and cuss and have no faith about it. So I can pay mine in faith, and you can pay yours in faith. But it's wrong thinking for you to say, "No, that's all my money." Well no, there wouldn't be a government and there wouldn't be a nation or a place for you to live. There wouldn't be freedom and protection. There wouldn't be all of the federal provisions, no Federal Reserve and no money. You didn't create all that by yourself, right?

The Things That Are God's

Jesus said, "Render unto Caesar what is his," but He didn't stop there. What was He saying? "If it's Caesar's, give what's Caesar's to Caesar. If it's the IRS's, give what's theirs to them. If it's God's, give what is His to Him." What is God's? Does God have any money? Is any of it His?

Some still say, "It's all His." Like I just said, that's wrong. And I know people don't believe it, because they don't act like it. They don't believe all the money in their possession is God's because they spend it like it's theirs. The problem is that many, many people act like God has none of their money—that none of it is His. They'll pay the government their portion because they have to. But as far as they're concerned, none of it is God's. And that is just not true.

Has the Bible said that a portion is God's? It has—from before the Law, during the Law, and after the Law.

The Things That Are God's

In Matthew 23:23, Jesus said, "Woe unto you, scribes and Pharisees, hypocrites! for ye pay tithe of mint and anise and cumin, and have omitted the weightier matters of the law, judgment, mercy, and faith: these ought ye to have done, and not to leave the other undone."

The Good News Translation says, "These you should practice, without neglecting the others." What should you practice? He didn't say, "That's silly. You don't need to tithe off of every little thing." He said you *should* do it.

The Living Bible says, "Yes, you should tithe, but you shouldn't leave the more important things undone," either.

Did Jesus say you should tithe? You hear people say, "Well, there's nothing about tithing in the New Testament." Is Matthew in the New Testament? Is Hebrews in the New Testament? Is Luke in the New Testament? And like we studied in chapter

1, is He going to give multiple chapters in the New Testament to something that doesn't even apply to us anymore? Why would He do that? And yet, that's what Hebrews is talking about—that whole passage.

Tithing is not just about keeping a rule; tithing is about honoring God and being blessed.

The only reason a person wouldn't like this is because they think it's someone trying to take something from them. Check your heart and see if you think I'm trying to trick or manipulate somebody into giving, or if it's about truth, about God's plan and way. Judge and see if you think I care about you or not. My biggest interest here is that you be blessed. God's way is good. His way is right. His way works. I want to see you prospering, flourishing, with everything paid off, and in the best shape of your life. I want to see all your needs met. I want to see your kids and grandkids flourishing and taken care of well. That's what this is about. And friend, tithing opens the door. It's not my idea. We will read about it in Malachi.

Malachi 3:6 starts by saying, "For I am the Lord," *and I switch things up regularly*. No. He changes not. And yet many have said, "No, we're not doing that anymore. He's changed." To listen to some people talk, you would think that way. But He does not change.

Everything God ever said is good and right and perfect and holy forever. He doesn't change. He doesn't need to change. We needed another way to be right with Him because we didn't—and couldn't—keep the Law. That's not a reflection on the Law; it's a reflection on us. *We* came short, not the Law. And thank God, Jesus came and kept the Law for us, and paid the price for us. He did it in our place. And now all we have to do to be right with God is have faith in Jesus.

That is one area, but that's not all there is in the Bible. There are a lot of other things to talk about. Even though we are justified by grace and by faith, we still have things we need to do. And we need to do them the way God wants us to do them, His ways of doing things.

He said, "For I am the Lord, I change not." Verse 7 continues, "Even from the days of your fathers ye are gone away from mine ordinances," you got away from what I told you, "and have not kept them. Return unto me, and I will return unto you." Another way of saying this is "give back to Me, return to Me, what is Mine. Give back to me, and I will give back to you." Now you know that's what it means because notice what they said. "Wherein shall we return?" They didn't say, "Okay, we'll come back." They said, "What are we going to give back? What are we going to return to You?" And He said, "Will a man rob God? Yet ye have robbed me. But ye say, Wherein have

The Things That Are God's

we robbed thee?" And He said, "In tithes and offerings." (v. 8)

Why are they asking, "What are we going to give back to You, and when did we take anything from You?" They're asking because they do not believe part of it is God's. They have gotten away from what He revealed through Abraham and Melchizedek. They've gotten away from what was given through Moses. They've just gotten away from it, like much of the Church today has gotten away from God and His things—and replaced it with what?

What replaced tithing? People say, "We just bring the sacrifice of praise now." They had praise then, too. "I just give as I am led." That's a wonderful idea, but who is it that is leading you? The Holy Spirit—the same One Who said these words in this Book—He's going to lead you contrary to what He's already said? Or He's going to lead you to do far less in this new and better covenant than they did in the old covenant?

The Things That Are God's

He's going to lead you to support the federal government much more than you support the Kingdom of God?

It's just an excuse. People say, "I'm just led," and then they do nothing or next to nothing. It's just not true; it's dishonest.

Now why would God say they robbed Him, unless He thinks part of that is His? God does think part of that is His. What do you think? Jesus said, "Give to Caesar what is Caesar's. Give to God what is God's." What is God's? Don't say, "All of it," because that can't be true. If all of it is God's, then none of it is Caesar's. None of it is yours. The Scripture is very clear. He said it numerous places—that the tithe belongs to the Lord.

Leviticus 27:30 is just one of several places that say it like this. "And all the tithe of the land, whether of the seed of the land, or of the fruit of the tree, is the LORD'S: it is holy unto the LORD." Then verse 32 says,

"And concerning the tithe of the herd, or the flock, even of whatsoever passeth under the rod, the tenth shall be holy unto the LORD."

Say this out loud: **The tithe belongs to the Lord.**

What did Jesus say? "Give to God what is God's."

The tithe is not an offering, because it wasn't yours. When you're tithing, you're not giving an offering, because it wasn't yours to give. You don't own the tithe. You are a steward of the tithe. Our stewardship is to return the tithe to Him.

Now, anything above the tithe was yours, right? So because it was yours, and you gave it to Him, it was a gift from you to Him, and He receives it as such.

It's sad that some people think it's a negative thing to talk about tithing, because this is some of the most wonderful shouting news you ever heard. He's telling them, "Give back to Me," and what will happen? "I will give back to you." Is there a reciprocity here? You give to Him, and He gives to you; you honor Him, and He honors you. Abraham honored Him, and He blessed Abraham.

He said, "You have robbed Me… in tithes and offerings." Verse 10 continues, "Bring ye all the tithes into the storehouse, that there may be meat" or food, provision, "in mine house…" I plan to talk about what that means—about where the tithe should go and how you should handle it—in the next chapter.

We have to do first things first, though. If you don't believe in tithing, there's no need to talk about the other parts.

Why did He say to bring all the tithes into the storehouse? So that there may be meat, or food, provision in His house. Does God have any money down here in this earth? Is all of it His? Obviously not. Now sure, by right of creation, the whole planet is His. By right of redemption, the whole planet is His. And eventually, in time to come, it's all going to be under His power and control. But right now, it's not all under His control. I know a lot of people don't like that phrase, but it's the truth.

In Psalm 115:16, it says, "The heaven, even the heavens, are the Lord's: but the earth hath he given to the children of men." When you really give something to someone, you don't call it yours anymore.

There are all kinds of people spending money on drug trafficking, human trafficking, genocide, and wars. Is that God's money? Is He doing that with His money? Absolutely not.

Well, does God have any money in this earth right now? Yes, He does, and it's the tithe of His people. That's His money.

The Things That Are God's

But, much of the church world is not tithing. And because of that, there is lack in the things of God. Many of His churches, ministries, and ministers are lacking sorely.

Just a couple of years ago, Phyllis and I were included in a meeting with the pastors and elders of a certain church. We didn't know them until a couple of days before the meeting, but through a series of events, we wound up sitting there with them. The pastor and his wife were crying. We didn't know what had happened; we just walked into this. It turned out they had just let all of their staff go because they could no longer pay them. There was no money to continue. And even though they had a good-sized congregation of people attending there, they were at the point of closing the place because of the unpaid bills and simply not enough funds.

Now there is no way that even half of those people were tithing and giving, with this kind of thing going on. So there are people,

The Things That Are God's

pastors, working multiple jobs, and they're worn-out when they take the pulpit. They're inadequately staffed, the staff is not paid decently, and the list goes on and on and on. I'm not saying that all of your tithe has to go to your local church, but if even half of the people tithed, and just half of their tithe went to their local church, there would be a great abundance of money. You know it's true. Consider it: if half the people who attended really tithed and just put half of their tithes in the local church, there would be so much money. Why did He say to bring the tithes? So there may be meat, food, and provision in My house.

Notice what happens if you do that. "And prove me now herewith… if I will not open you the windows of heaven, and pour you out a blessing, that there shall not be room enough to receive it." (Malachi 3:10) Is this the Word of God? Is it true? This is not Law. This is the Prophets, but even if it was the Law, the Law is still good and holy and right.

God doesn't change. Isn't that what He said in verse 6? I don't change. Is He the same today as He was with Abraham? What did Abraham do? He honored God. He couldn't send the money and things to God personally in heaven, so he gave it to God's high priest, who is representing Him. And God doesn't need US dollars in heaven, right? He doesn't need anything material or natural or substance-wise in heaven. But do His people need things down here in the earth? Do His ministries, His churches, His outreaches, His missions, and His ministers need things down here? Well, does God have any money down here? Yes. It's the tithe. The tithes of every one of His people is His.

And this is not about Him getting something from us. This is His way of operating and functioning, and He said if you will do this, "I will open the windows of heaven." (v. 10) Now a window is an opening. And just like the rain comes out of the atmospheric heaven and waters the seed

The Things That Are God's

and causes the crops to grow and the harvest to be abundant, the same way the blessing—the "rain" of blessing—comes down on the tither. Because you tithed, it gave God access into your affairs—an opening, a window into your life.

Would you like God to be involved in your business? Well, how do you get Him in your business? This has always been His way. Did God get involved in Abraham's business? Yes, He did.

You bring the tithes, "that there may be food in mine house, and prove me now herewith," He says, "if I will not open you the windows of heaven, and pour you out a blessing, that there shall not be room enough to receive it." You will run out of room because you are so blessed.

Leviticus says you'll have to take out the old store because of the new. (Leviticus 26:10) You'll have to take the two-year-old car out of your garage because the new one has to go in there. You'll have to take those last-year clothes out because you have so many new clothes. And we don't just need to find a place to stockpile them because we're givers. We're sowers. Somebody else is going to enjoy driving that two-year-old car. Why? Because we are so blessed, we don't have room to store it all.

Didn't it come to pass in Abraham's life just like this? He was a tither. He gave tithes of all to Melchizedek, who is the forerunner of Jesus, our High Priest, and Melchizedek blessed him because he was authorized to receive his tithes and was anointed to bless him.

The Bible says Abraham had so many cows, so much gold, and so much silver that the land could not contain them. They did not have room to receive it.

If you say, "I don't believe in tithing," then you don't believe in this either, right? You can't separate them.

The Things That Are God's

It's so sad that people get very indignant, irritated, and aggravated about tithing. This blessing is what they are fighting. It's like people who get so up in arms and resist speaking in tongues. Do they have any clue what they're fighting? Or it's like people who fight prosperity. Why?! Or they fight healing and miracles and faith. That just shows a lack of understanding.

Well, it's the same way here. Why would you fight God having access into your material affairs and blessing you until you run out of room? Why would you fight God rebuking the devourer off of you and your stuff? Why would you fight that? These blessings belong to the tither.

Say this out loud: **Tithing is giving to God what is God's. Tithing is honoring God and giving Him access. Tithing is provision and protection.**

Do you believe that's in the Bible? Is that true or not? It was revealed in Abraham, confirmed in the Law and prophets, confirmed by Jesus Himself, and has chapters given to it in the New Testament, in Hebrews. Don't say tithing is not for us today. Don't say it has passed away. That's just simply not true.

If you want to see my wife get stirred up, you'll see it with her acting on this verse about the devourer being rebuked. She's quick to quote this one! A while back, something we had recently gotten failed, and we were told it was going to cost us thousands of dollars to replace it. Immediately Phyllis jumped up and said, "No! No! The devourer is rebuked. The devourer is rebuked!" It was something that wasn't very old, and we shouldn't be having to spend money on it. She said, "No, no, we're tithers! The devourer is rebuked." She went on for a couple of minutes. "The devourer is rebuked. He can't take our money. He can't steal our money." You know, we didn't do anything. We just put that on hold, and within a couple of days, we received a different report that it could be easily restored at no cost to us. We didn't have to spend that money; we didn't need to. Our money wasn't devoured.

I have seen that over and over and over again. What is the devourer? It's the destroyer. It's the enemy, the consumer. It's something that tries to eat up your prosperity and your plenty.

"Be sober, be vigilant; because your adversary the devil, as a roaring lion, walketh about, seeking whom he may devour." (1 Peter 5:8)

It's not enough to just make more money and increase. You can make twice as much money as you have been making, but if you get hit with expenses and losses that are three times what you have been making, you're still in the hole. You not only need increase, which is what the windows of heaven and the blessing is about, but you also need protection. I said, "You need protection." You need your things protected from the devourer, and God has access and a right to do it when you honor Him and tithe.

I don't know about you, but I'm going to keep on tithing. I have made up my mind. I am fully persuaded about this.

In verse 11, He said, "And I will rebuke the devourer for your sakes, and he shall not destroy the fruits of your ground; neither shall your vine cast her fruit before the time in the field, saith the LORD of hosts." Now don't just get stuck on the agrarian examples; this applies to you. This talks about you investing into something and then nothing coming of it, which means all your time and money was just devoured. You're working on a deal, working on a deal, working on a deal, and then nothing comes of it. You wind up being in the hole. That's not being blessed. That's being devoured. And if you're a tither, God said, "I'm going to rebuke," *God* is going to rebuke, "the devourer" off of you and your things. Why? Why doesn't He do it for everybody? He said He does it for tithers. So you won't lose things, and things won't be cut off before their time. Things won't be consumed and destroyed, and you will be protected.

The reason these things won't happen for everyone is because many will not give God any place in their lives. It's only when we acknowledge Him and yield to Him in honor, faith, and obedience that He has an opening to do it for us.

He continues in verse 12, "And all nations shall call you blessed." Think about it. What if the majority of this country tithed? What if the United States of America was a tithing country? I tell you what, it wouldn't take long for our finances to get straightened out, and we would be protected. So whether it's a nation, or whether it's a family or a church or an individual, it's all the same. We need to

The Things That Are God's

honor God, and we need His blessing and His protection. God has given us tithing as the blessing connector, and as the protection connector, because faith without works is dead. It can't all be just idle talk.

Tithing is a lot like praying. Why don't a lot of people pray? It's for the same reason they don't tithe. For one thing, a lot of folks are not that convinced that God is even real, or that He even exists. Or they think if He is real, would He actually hear the prayer, and *what good would it do?*

Read the rest of this section. In verse 13, He said, "Your words have been stout against me, saith the LORD. Yet ye say, What have we spoken so much against thee?" Can you tell these folks are clueless? To just about everything He says, they ask, "What? What? What are You talking about?"

He said, "When are you going to give what is Mine back to Me?"

The Things That Are God's

And they say, "What? What? What do You mean?"

He said, "What are all these things you've been saying against Me?"

And they say, "What? What? What did we say?" Just because you play dumb doesn't mean it's not happening.

Look at the end of verse 13 again. "Yet ye say, What have we spoken so much against thee? Ye have said, It is vain to serve God: and what profit is it that we have kept his ordinance…?" (v. 14) He originally talked about the ordinances they had forsaken, that involved tithing and giving. So He's saying, "I heard you when you said, 'It doesn't do any good to tithe. It doesn't help anybody to give offerings. It doesn't do any good to go to church or pray, or do any of those things. That's just fools being fooled.'" He said, "Those words are stout against Me."

The Things That Are God's

I don't want to say any stout words against God, do you? No. I believe it is not vain to serve God. It benefits us; it pays to serve God. It pays to pray. It pays to come to church. It pays to tithe and give. It pays to give offerings. It pays to serve God. I'm not going to speak against Him. I'm going to agree with Him.

You have to be like Phyllis. You have to be ready to spring up and declare, "No! The devourer is rebuked! He can't steal my stuff. Why? I'm a tither. I'm a tither." And we're so glad we can say that about the churches. Faith Life Church is a tithing church, and we're a blessed church. And we're a protected church. It's not because we were so smart and did everything so perfectly. It's because God is watching over us. There is an opening where blessing rain is coming through on us, and God Himself is rebuking the devourer and destroyer off of us.

Abraham, Isaac, and Jacob were tithers. Moses and Aaron, David, and the patriarchs of generations were tithers. Jesus was a tither. Phyllis and I have made up our minds; we and our churches and ministers are tithers. Don't you want to be a tither too?

Chapter 3: Honor and Blessing

If you're a serious believer in God and want His will and way in your life, pray this prayer before Him.

Prayer: *Father, in the Name of Jesus, I ask You to help me rise above man's traditions and religious ideas, and above any wrong thinking, any preconceived notions that never were You and are in disagreement with Your Holy Word. Help me to see Your truth, not man's ideas and opinions. Help me to see what pleases You and is your perfect will for me today, in the New Covenant. Help me to see how all of Your truth applies to me and how to walk in the light of it.*

Any changes I need to make, I ask You to show me. If there's anything I've not known, reveal it to me. If I've let slip what You've shown me, show me again, please. Anything I need to start or stop or change, I ask You for it, and I'm willing to do it as You help me, in Jesus' Name. Amen.

Hebrews 7:7 says, "And without all contradiction the less is blessed of the better. And here men that die receive tithes; but there he receiveth them, of whom it is witnessed that He liveth. And as I may so say, Levi also, who receiveth tithes, payed tithes in Abraham." (vv. 7-9)

In the previous two chapters, we covered a lot of ground on tithing. We dealt with the idea that tithing is just part of the Law and not for us today—which is completely untrue and unscriptural. After all, we're reading in Hebrews, in the New Testament. And then we went into a lot of detail about what tithing is.

We saw that Melchizedek met Abraham after the great victory they had over the enemy kings and their armies, where he recovered Lot and his family and all the people and possessions from those cities. It was a miracle. Melchizedek is the high priest of God, but we have no record of his origins; he's not of the seed of Aaron. This was way before Moses got the Law, pre-Law.

We know Abraham learned how to walk by faith and was justified by faith—just like we are—long before there was any kind of a law to observe. He also learned how to tithe. Where did he get it from? It wasn't a rule, it wasn't a law, there was no statute, and there was no ordinance. He got it from God. And why did he do it? He did it out of honor. He was honoring the God Who just saved his life and gave them victory and brought them back with all their possessions. And in response to such graciousness and faithfulness from God, the Bible says he gave Melchizedek tithes of everything. "Tithe" means "ten percent."

Why did Abraham give 10%? Why not 5% or 50%? Was it just a random percentage he came up with? Or did He get this percentage from God, in keeping with the rest of the scriptures that the tenth has always belonged to God?

Hebrews 7 goes into detail, saying Melchizedek was a type of our High Priest, Jesus. Verse 8 says, "And here men that die receive tithes, but there He receiveth them, of whom it is witnessed that he liveth." Our High Priest Jesus lives. All of the Aaronic priests are gone, long gone, but Jesus lives. Do you think He still receives tithes? Well, yes. This is unchanged. This was before the Law, during, and after the Law. Just like faith is before, during, and after the Law. It's the same thing.

Where should the tithe go? Now that's the ten-million-dollar question, isn't it? This is where people part ways in their thinking. Where is the tithe supposed to go?

Leviticus 27:30 says, "And all the tithe of the land, whether of the seed of the land, or of the fruit of the tree, is the LORD'S: it is holy unto the LORD."

Now, I guess I need to say this again. Some say, "Well, Brother Keith, that's Leviticus. That doesn't apply to us." I just read verses in Hebrews. I'll give you numerous other New Testament scriptures that link together with this.

There's a big problem in the body about despising the Old Testament. It's a failure to understand. The Holy Spirit speaking through the writers of the New Testament refer to the Old Testament hundreds of times. Have you not noticed that? Why would they do that if it's not relevant anymore, or if it doesn't apply to us anymore?

Sacrifice for sin has been fulfilled, but everything God has ever said is still true and right and good. We understand the Old Testament in light of the New Testament, but the New makes repeated reference to the Old. So if you don't know the Old, you're not going to understand many things in the New. If all you know is the Old Testament, you won't be enlightened to what has happened since then. You will be stuck there. So you need both. You have both an Old and New Testament in your Bible, and you're not going to throw any of it away, right? I will show you New Testament scriptures that tie right into what we're reading here in Leviticus.

Read verse 30 again. "And all the tithe of the land, whether of the seed of the land, or of the fruit of the tree, is the LORD'S: it is holy unto the LORD." Verse 32 repeats the idea. It says, "…the tenth shall be holy unto the Lord."

In Malachi 3:6, it says, "For I am the Lord, I change not…" Does God change? No, He doesn't change.

Our approach to Him has changed from the Old Testament in that we don't cover our sins every year with animal blood. The Blood of the Lamb has washed us once and for all. And yet, God hasn't changed. Our access to Him has changed, but He hasn't changed. He didn't need to change, and He never will.

He said, "For I am the Lord, I change not; therefore ye sons of Jacob are not consumed. Even from the days of your fathers ye are gone away from mine ordinances…" We just read one of the things He told them, that the tithe belongs to the Lord, and this is what He's talking about. He said, "…and [you] have not kept them. Return unto me, and I will return unto you." Now some may try to translate that as "come back to Me, and I'll come back to you," but no, it's "return what is Mine back to Me, and I will return to you." I guess both could be true if you're coming back to God, then you're going to give back to God what is God's. The end of verse 7 continues, "But ye said, Wherein shall we return?" What will we return back to You?

Verse 8 says. "Will a man rob God? Yet ye have robbed me. But ye say, Wherein have we robbed thee? In tithes and offerings." Does God believe that the tithe is His? What do you think?

In the previous chapters, I asked the question, "Is any of the money down here God's?" Many people say, "It's all His," but that's not true. If it's all His, why do people keep treating it like it's all theirs? And if it's all His, then we would have nothing to give Him, ever. Anything we would give Him is already His, so we could never give Him an offering. It's not true. It's a religious tradition, a notion. It sounds good to people, but it's not true. All of it is not His.

In Psalm 115:16, it says, "The heaven, even the heavens, are the Lord's: but the earth hath he given to the children of men." He gave men the earth, right? And all of it. He doesn't say that it's His. It is His by right of creation, and ultimately it's going to wind up under His control, but as it stands right now, if you say, "All the money and everything down here is His," then a lot of God's money is being used for bad things.

Does God have a portion that is His? What is it? It's the tithe. God has said repeatedly that the tenth part is His.

Years ago, I asked the Lord where the tithe goes, because I was studying—for everything I was worth—to see how I might understand this. I wanted to know where it is supposed to go, because I've seen people get heated (even preachers almost coming to blows) over this question about where the tithe goes. I asked Him, "Lord, who does the tithe belong to?"

And immediately the answer was strong inside me. He said, "The tithe is Mine. The tithe is Mine."

Say that out loud: **The Lord said the tenth part belongs to Him.**

Some people say, "All the tithe belongs to the local church." So is the local church the Lord? Now granted, if you go to a church where you get fed, where you get helped, and where your family gets ministered to, certainly at least some (and even a lot) of your tithes should go there. Certainly. But to rigidly, legalistically demand that 100% of your tithes has to go and can only go to that local church, what scripture is that based on?

It is important to remember that in the new Covenant, nothing is to be done just as a ritual or routine. Everything is to be done in love, in faith, and by the direction of the Holy Spirit.

"Now the end of the commandment is charity out of a pure heart, and of a good conscience, and of faith unfeigned:"
(1 Timothy 1:5)

"For as many as are led by the Spirit of God, they are the sons of God." (Romans 8:14)

If you always subtract exactly 10% and pay it like a bill to the same place mechanically, you never need to pray about it, and there's no need to be led by the Spirit. But if the tithe really belongs to the Lord, shouldn't we inquire of Him day to day as to where He wants it to go, and how He wants it administered?

Some have even paid tithes as though it were protection money. They did it out of fear, trying to "keep God happy," so they don't get destroyed. That's not honor and thankfulness; that's not tithing.

This is also why no one should "require" anyone to tithe to them. If one is paying 10% like a mandatory bill because they have to, that's not honoring God; that's not tithing. We're told in 2 Corinthians 9:7, in the New International Version, **"Each of you should give what you have decided in** your heart to give, **not reluctantly or under compulsion**, for God loves a cheerful giver."

For if the willingness is there, the gift is acceptable according to what one has, not according to what he does not have. (2 Corinthians 8:12, NIV)

Compulsory, mandatory tithing or giving is unscriptural in the New Testament. And it couldn't be acceptable to God if it's not done willingly out of love and in faith.

"But without faith it is impossible to please him…" (Hebrews 11:6)

"…but faith which worketh by love." (Galatians 5:6)

In Malachi 3:6, He said, "I don't change," and He went on to talk about them returning to Him. Then in verse 8 He told them, "You've robbed Me in tithes and offerings." Well, the only way they could have robbed Him was if the tithes and offerings were His. We need to get this settled once and for all. Don't just try to take my word for it and see if you agree with me or not. If you're not sure, read and study the Old and New Testament until you can get settled for yourself. Does the tithe belong to Him or not? If it's His, then you shouldn't just do what you want to do with it. It's not yours.

In our churches *(to provoke thought)*, I've asked the people *(though we wouldn't do it)*, "Do you think it would be ok for Phyllis and I as the pastors to take some of the church's building fund money and maybe go on a big vacation or buy ourselves some new cars with it?" Oh, you immediately hear strong disapproval and a resounding "Noooo!" So clearly everyone feels quite strongly that we ministers should not treat God's money like it's our own.

Well, if it's not ok for ministers to misappropriate funds, why is it ok for the people in the congregation to do that? To

Honor and Blessing

take God's money and spend it just like it's theirs? It's quite the double standard, don't you think?

He continues in verse 9. "Ye are cursed with a curse: for ye have robbed me, even this whole nation. Bring ye all the tithes into the storehouse…" Now this begins to tell you where the tithe goes. Some people have said, "That means 'the storehouse' is the local church." Well, where are your scripture verses to prove that?

If you bring the tithes in, to what purpose, to what end? "…that there may be meat," or food or provision, "in mine house…" (vv. 9-10) What is the Lord's house? The tithe supports the Lord's house. Bring all the tithes in, so that My house may be fully supplied. But what is the Lord's house?

If you do that, is there any benefit to you, the tither? He said, "Prove me now herewith… if I will not open you the windows of heaven, and pour you out a blessing, that there shall not be room enough to receive it."

People have thought so wrongly about tithing. Some say, "Do we have to tithe?" No, and you don't *have* to pray, either. You don't *have* to go to church. You don't *have* to do anything. They say, "I don't like being under some kind of law." This is not about a law. This is tithing, like Abraham did. He had no law. He had no rule. It's about honoring God.

It's about honoring God and giving Him access to bless you.

Do you know what a window is? A window is an opening that allows access. Tithing gives God access into our affairs. Access to do what? To bless us until there's not enough room to receive it. And what else? I like this "and." "And I [God] will rebuke the devourer for your sakes, and he shall not destroy the fruits of your ground; neither shall your vine cast her fruit before the time in the field, says the Lord of hosts." (v. 11) It's blessing and protection.

Say this out loud: **Blessing and protection.**

Didn't the Lord say, "Them that honour me I will honour?" (1 Samuel 2:30) *If* you honor the Lord. Proverbs talks about this in chapter 3. "Honour the Lord with thy substance, and with the firstfruits of all thine increase: So shall thy barns be filled with plenty, and thy presses shall burst out with new wine." (vv. 9-10)

When other people are losing their things, and you get to pay yours off and keep them, is that not God honoring you? When your needs are met, and other people had to close their business, and you opened up a new branch, that is God honoring you. Do you want God to honor you? Well, it's not just automatic or because you asked Him to.

It wouldn't be fair for God to do things for you that He's not doing for everyone else,

<u>unless</u> you're willing and glad to do something they refuse to do. Acknowledge and honor Him.

You have to honor Him, and in response to you honoring Him, He has a right, He has a window, He has an opening. He has an entrance and access to you—to bless you and to pour out blessing until you run out of room for it. And when the devourer is trying to steal your possessions and mess them up, God Himself says, "No you don't! No you don't!" You have to like that. You've got to like that God said, "*I* will rebuke the devourer for your sake." Who wouldn't like that? Of course, if you don't believe in tithing, none of this applies to you.

This is very important. So many people are confused about it, but the entrance of His Word gives light and gives understanding to the simple.

The Lord said, "Bring all the tithe into the storehouse that there may be" food, meat, provision "in My house." (Malachi 3:10) Who does the tithe belong to? Him. The tithe belongs to the Lord. What's the purpose of the tithe? That there may be provision in His house. Do you agree with that so far?

In Acts 7:44, we begin to see some things about the Lord's house. "Our fathers had the tabernacle of witness in the wilderness, as he had appointed, speaking unto Moses, that he should make it according to the fashion that he had seen. Which also our fathers that came after brought in with Jesus," or we would say *Joshua*, "into the possession of the Gentiles, whom God drave out before the face of our fathers, unto the days of David; Who found favour before God, and desired to find a tabernacle for the God of Jacob." (vv. 44-46) He has referred to two things now: first, the tabernacle, and then after that was the temple.

When the tabernacle was constructed, and especially when the temple was built, that was *the* house of God. It was the *only* house of God, and when He's talking about bringing the tithes into the storehouse, the storehouses were connected to that *one* structure.

Verse 47 continues, "But Solomon built him an house." That's the temple. First there was the tabernacle, then there was the temple. "Howbeit the most High dwelleth not in temples made with hands; as saith the prophet…" You know, sometimes we talk about how good it is to be in the house of the Lord. Well, if you're talking about the building, you're a little unscriptural. It's His in the sense that He gave it to us, and we dedicated it to Him, and we use it for His purposes, but no building or structure is the house God *lives* in. Why would He be in it? Because we're in it.

He said, "Heaven is my throne, and the earth is my footstool." (Isaiah 66:1) Now that's a picture, isn't it? How about the planet? Can you picture God with His feet on planet Earth? Earth is His footstool. He was asking, *What kind of house are you going to build for Me? My throne is in heaven. Earth is like My footstool. What kind of house are you going to build Me?*

"Where is the place of my rest? For all those things hath mine hand made…" (v. 2) We see that the house of God used to be one building. But is that the case today? So when He said to bring all of the tithes into the storehouse, He was talking about one building: *The* temple. We know that has changed. There's not *one* building where everybody has to go for church or to worship God, and the Lord has revealed to us now in the New Testament that He doesn't live in buildings made with men's hands. (Acts 7:48; 17:24)

Have we not understood from 1 Corinthians 3:16 and other places that *we* are the temple of the living God? He dwells in *us*.

Hebrews 3:6 says, "But Christ as a son over his own house; whose house are we…"

First Peter 2:5 says we are "…as lively stones, are built up a spiritual house, an holy priesthood, to offer up spiritual sacrifices, acceptable to God by Jesus Christ."

Do you believe we've been made kings and priests unto our God? Do you believe we are His spiritual house that He dwells in? Well then, do you also believe that as a priest, you and I are supposed to be offering up sacrifices? Is that true too? Yes, it is.

In 1 Timothy 3:15, he said, "But if I tarry long, that thou mayest know how thou oughtest to behave thyself in the house of God, which is the church of the living God, the pillar and ground of the truth."

He had said in Malachi, "Bring all the tithes into the storehouse that there may be meat in mine house." (3:10) Well, one building is

Honor and Blessing

not His house today. Do you agree with that?

We need to see New Testament truth and light, and we need to see the Old Testament precedent that is referred to in the New Testament. The New Testament is continually referring to the Old Testament precedent, because what God gave in the tabernacle, in the temple, in the priesthood, in the sacrifices and offerings, is a pattern right out of heaven. In heaven, there is a Holy of Holies, a real one. There are the angels over it. There is a Mercy Seat just like it was when He gave the pattern to Moses and then the pattern to David to build the temple. The real thing is in heaven. We'll get to see it soon. So do you think it would be foolish to read some of the descriptions of it in the Old Testament and scoff at it? What are you making light of or fun of? It's describing the real thing in heaven. And God doesn't change—did you remember that part? He doesn't change. He doesn't *need* to change.

Now, with that in mind, we will read Deuteronomy 14:22 in the New International Version. I think you can tell that I'm just hitting the high points, so if you really are interested in this, take the time and read these whole chapters, and let the Lord speak to you through them.

Deuteronomy 14:22 says, "Be sure to set aside a tenth of all that your fields produce each year." (NIV) Continue reading verse 23 in the KJV. "And thou shalt eat before the Lord thy God, in the place which he shall choose to place his name there, the tithe of thy corn, of thy wine, and of thine oil, and the firstlings of thy herds and of thy flocks; that thou mayest learn to fear the Lord thy God always."

Skip down to verse 27. "And the Levite that is within thy gates; thou shalt not forsake him; for he hath no part nor inheritance with thee. At the end of three years thou shalt bring forth all the tithe of thine increase the same year, and shalt lay it up within thy gates." (vv. 27-28) Where do you lay it up? Within *your* gates. Is that right? That's what it says. "And the Levite, (because he hath no part nor inheritance with thee,) and the stranger, and the fatherless, and the widow, which are within thy gates, shall come, and **shall** eat and be satisfied; that the Lord thy God may bless thee in all the work of thine hand which thou doest." (v. 29) They're going to eat of what? The tithe.

Now there are many more scriptures than the ones I'm sharing with you, but these are, to me, some of the most clear.

Deuteronomy 26:12 in the NIV says, "When you have finished setting aside a tenth of all your produce in the third year, the year of the tithe, you shall give it to the Levite, the foreigner, the fatherless and the widow." He mentions the four categories where the tithe goes. Are we answering the question that asks where the tithe goes? "…give it to the Levite, the foreigner, the fatherless and the widow, so that they may eat in your towns and be satisfied." Then verse 13 says, "Then say to the Lord your God: 'I have removed from my house the sacred portion and have given it to the Levite, the foreigner, the fatherless and the widow, according to all you commanded.'" This is the third time we've read this. "'I have not turned aside from your commands nor have I forgotten any of them. I have not eaten any of the sacred portion while I was in mourning, nor have I removed any of it while I was unclean, nor have I offered any of it to the dead.'" (vv. 13-14) You're not supposed to dip into the tithes if times gets hard, or if you get pressed. You don't dip into the tithes. Then he says in verse 15, "Look down from heaven, your holy dwelling place, and bless your people Israel and the land you have given us as you promised on oath to our ancestors, a land flowing with milk and honey." Is tithing always connected with blessing? Always.

So, the Old Testament precedent, which just means "that which preceded," reveals that the tithe went to the Levites, and it went to the stranger or alien, and it went to the fatherless and the widow.

Now strangers, the fatherless, and widows are similar. A "stranger" meant somebody who is displaced, who is not in their own country and not with their own family. They need help. Maybe they don't have a job, and they don't have a place to live. And a similar idea was with the fatherless and widows, God's people who are in need and are in lack. Can tithes go to this? Well, if you say, "No," what scripture are you basing that on? You only have two sources for belief: what men think and what God said. So concerning anything you think you believe or know about this, question yourself, examine yourself, and ask, "What scripture do I have for that? Where is that?" I don't care if you've always done it that way, or if your grandma did, or if your denomination or group did, what scripture did they have? Don't you think we ought to examine these things by the scriptures? Certainly we should.

So we see two basic groups that the tithe was to go to: those in need—genuine need—and the Levites.

Levites are part of the ministry. The ministry consisted of both priests and Levites, and the Levites were the ones that did what we would call "the ministry of helps," or all of the natural work. They set up the tabernacle and broke it down, and they carried it, and they manned the fires, and they cleaned up after the sacrifices. It takes a lot of natural work for the church and the ministry to operate. This would be like our church and ministry staffs doing the natural work of the ministry today.

And then the priests were the ones who represented God to the people and the people to God, the ones who actually performed the sacrifices. The high priest went into the Holy of Holies with the blood and made atonement, and the priests who directed the activities of the house of God and read and taught the Law and prophets would be comparable to our five-fold ministry gifts today, the speaking gifts. The priests are a type of the apostles, prophets, evangelists, pastors, and teachers we have today. Our current ministers and ministry of helps are typified by the priests and Levites.

You might say, "What does all of this Old Testament Scripture have to do with us?" It has everything to do with us. I'm going to show you from the New Testament why we know this.

In Deuteronomy 18:1, it says, "The priests the Levites, and all the tribe of Levi, shall have no part nor inheritance with Israel: they shall eat the offerings of the Lord made by fire, and his inheritance. Therefore shall they have no inheritance among their brethren: the Lord is their inheritance, as he hath said unto them. And this shall be the priest's due from the people, from them that offer a sacrifice, whether it be ox or sheep; and they shall give unto the priest the shoulder, and the two cheeks, and the maw. The firstfruit also of thy corn, of thy wine, and of thine oil, and the first of the fleece of thy sheep, shalt thou give him. For the Lord thy God hath chosen him out of all thy tribes, to stand to minister in the name of the Lord, him and his sons for ever." (vv. 1-5)

The priests and the Levites were not given any land to inherit. We read in the Book of Joshua that even though the first generation didn't come in and take the promised land, under Joshua's leadership the next generation did. And as they won victories, they divided specific portions to each of the twelve tribes. Well, the priests and Levites did not get an allotment of land. That meant they couldn't have crops and couldn't have herds, and basically, they didn't have business like the other people did. So how were they going to live? How were they going to make it? Well, the Lord ordained—and this is quoted in the New Testament, in 1 Corinthians 9:13-14: "Do ye not know that they which minister about holy things live of the things of the temple? and they which wait at the altar are partakers with the altar?" "Even so hath the Lord ordained that they which preach the gospel should live of the gospel."

The priests and Levites were to be sustained by the tithes and offerings of God's people, and in the very same way, New Testament ministers are to be provided for by the tithes and offerings of His people. Is that right? Isn't 1 Corinthians for us today?

Actually, there are numerous offerings mentioned in the Scriptures. Have you ever read about all of them, in Leviticus, Numbers, Deuteronomy, all of those places? There was of course the offerings for sin, and some of those were whole burnt offerings—and we know that doesn't apply to us anymore because Jesus is our final Sacrifice for sin. But there were also thank offerings and peace offerings. Could you give an offering today because you are thankful? Certainly you can. And there were tithes, and there were firstfruits. They had an offering every year called the "half shekel offering," and that just went to the upkeep of the temple. That wasn't connected to anything else. They had several offerings, but they were not tithes.

The priests and the Levites received a portion of a lot of the people's offerings. If you look at all of the offerings they received, plus the tithes, plus the firstfruits, they had to be well off. There's a lot coming in to them, so they had to be well off. Don't just take my word for it. You'll have to study a little bit, but go back and look at all the offerings they received. They had a lot of things coming in to them, all the time. Their mainstay was the tithe. Deuteronomy 12:19 in the Amplified Bible, Classic Edition says, "Take heed not to forsake *or* neglect the Levite [God's minister] as long as you live in your land."

He said, "Don't neglect them." Why? They don't have land. They don't have crops. They don't have herds. So if you don't tithe, if you don't give, their needs are not going to be met. They are part of the operation of the house of the Lord. Do you see this? They weren't supposed to be working crops and tending herds. They were supposed to be giving themselves full-time to the ministry that the Lord had for them there. And the tithes and offerings enabled them to do that.

Do you believe God could prosper us no matter what's happening in the economy or in the world around us? Do you believe it? No matter what's going on, you and I could still increase year after year?

One might say, "Well, I just lost everything." It's the perfect time for you to get something new! And launch into an area you have never been before. But do you know what you're going to need in order to be able to do that in this harsh, cruel world?

You're going to need the blessing. You're going to need God's blessing. And with His empowering, enabling, protecting blessing, you can make it through anything. Do you believe that? With His blessing, you can accomplish anything.

He said in Numbers 18:21, "I give to the Levites all the tithes in Israel as their inheritance in return for the work they do while serving at the tent of meeting." (NIV) So the tithe is the Lord's, but you can't send it to heaven, right? So in the temple worship and the tabernacle worship, who was receiving the tithes? The priests and the Levites were getting them.

Verse 22 continues, "From now on the Israelites must not go near the tent of meeting, or they will bear the consequences of their sin and die."

Skip down to verse 26. "Speak to the Levites and say to them: 'When you receive from the Israelites the tithe I give you as your inheritance, you must present a tenth of that tithe as the Lord's offering." Should preachers tithe too? Yes—and churches and ministries. Who shouldn't tithe? Everybody should tithe. Well, who wants to be blessed? Who wants to be protected and kept? He said, "Speak to the Levites and say to them: 'When you receive from the Israelites the tithe I give you as your inheritance, you must present a tenth of that tithe as the Lord's offering. Your offering will be reckoned to you as grain from the threshing floor or juice from the winepress." (vv. 26-27) They don't have farms, they don't have herds, they don't have flocks, and they don't have businesses, but they *can* tithe off of the tithes. Can you see that? Who did that tithe go to?

Verse 28 says, "In this way you also will present an offering to the Lord from all the tithes you receive…. From these tithes you must give the Lord's portion to Aaron the priest." This would be comparable to the preachers of our day. They had the Levites, the helps ministry, and Aaron and his sons were the priests. So the tithe of the tithe went to the priests. The Levites were paid out of the tithes, then the tithe of the tithes went to the priests. Can you see this? "You must present as the Lord's portion the best and holiest part of everything given to you. Say to the Levites: 'When you present the best part, it will be reckoned to you as the product of the threshing floor or the winepress." (vv. 29-30)

We read in the New Testament, in Hebrews 7:9, where he said, "Levi also, who receiveth tithes, payed tithes in Abraham."

If you receive tithes, you should also tithe yourself.

And we read in verse 7 that "the less is blessed of the greater," showing that Melchizedek was greater, in a sense, than Abraham because when Abraham tithed, Melchizedek blessed him; honor and blessing.

Honor and Blessing

Let me give you some more scripture verses. In the mouth of two or three witnesses, or three or four or five, let every Word be established. Are you in agreement with this?

You will see in Nehemiah that the people had gotten away from God. They quit tithing, and they quit giving, which always happens when God's people backslide. When people get cold, one of the first things that stops is the giving. Then when people are revived, and they get close to God, that's one of the first things that starts happening again—the giving.

This is not only in the Old Testament. Do you remember the Book of Acts, when they all got filled with the Holy Spirit? What happened immediately? In the very next chapter, it said that none of them lacked because everybody was giving. They were selling houses and buildings and lands, right? And they were sowing to the point that everybody had their needs met. Can you imagine a church of thousands and thousands of people, and not one of them had any unmet needs? Is that possible again today? Well, that's what happens when people get full of the Spirit and get full of love and faith. But the colder you are, the stingier you are, and the less you want to give, the more you want to argue about whether or not you *have to* give. That shows coldness and a lack of spirituality.

In Nehemiah 10:35, he said, "Bring the firstfruits of our ground, and the firstfruits of all fruit of all trees, year by year, unto the house of the Lord." Then in verse 37, he said, "And that we should bring the firstfruits of our dough, and our offerings, and the fruit of all manner of trees, of wine and of oil, unto the priests, to the chambers of the house of our God; and the tithes of our ground unto the Levites, that the same Levites might have the tithes in all the cities of our tillage. And the priest the son of Aaron shall be with the Levites, when the Levites take tithes: and the Levites shall bring up the tithe of the tithes unto the house of our God, to the chambers, into the treasure house. For the children of Israel and the children of Levi shall bring the offering of the corn, of the new wine, and the oil, unto the chambers, where are the vessels of the sanctuary, and the priests that minister, and the porters, and the singers: and **we will not forsake the house of our God**." (vv. 35-39) Tithing is supporting the house of God so that there may be plenty of provision in His house.

Nehemiah 12:44 says, "And at that time were there some appointed over the chambers for the treasures, for the offerings, for the firstfruits, and for the tithes, to gather them out of the fields of the cities the portions of the law for the priests and Levites: for Judah rejoiced for the priests and for the Levites that waited." They valued the priests and Levites. Some of the Levites were singers, some of them carried the articles of the Temple, some of them got the wood and kept the fires going, some of them cleaned the place, and of course, the priests were handling the Law and were officiating over the sacrifices. The tithes, among other offerings, and the tithes of tithes were going to these people. "And both the singers and the porters kept the ward of their God…. For in the days of David and Asaph of old there were chief of the singers, and songs of praise and thanksgiving to God. And all Israel in the days of Zerubbabel, and in the days of Nehemiah, gave the portions of the singers and the porters, every day his portion: and they sanctified holy things unto the Levites; and the Levites sanctified them to the children of Aaron." (vv. 44-47) That means "set apart."

Do you think there are many churches today that are understaffed, and the few staff there are underpaid, sometimes working multiple jobs just to make ends meet? That is not right. Why is it that way? Because the people are not tithing and not giving; there isn't food and provision in

God's house. There is lack, and there is shortage. People say, "I don't go by any rules. I just give as I'm led by the Spirit to." Now, I think being led by the Spirit is one of the most important things there is in the life of the believer, but I don't believe that the Holy Spirit is going to lead you to do something contrary to what He's already revealed in His word, or to do less under this new and better covenant than they did under the old covenant. No, if a believer is consistently putting less than ten percent of their increase into the Kingdom of God, they're not putting the Kingdom first, and they're not being led by the Holy Spirit.

And it's not a matter of "can't afford to," it's a matter of priorities and faith. You have to make a commitment. It's not about doing it to the church, it's about doing it unto the Lord. It's His tithe, so you put it where *He* says.

In Nehemiah 13, this ungodly individual came in, and they prepared a chamber for him where the Levites, the singers, and the offerings were supposed to be; they kicked them out. In verse 10, Nehemiah said, "And I perceived that the portions of the Levites had not been given them…" We talked about this earlier. Does God have a portion that is His? Do the ministers have a portion that is theirs? "…for the Levites and the singers, that did the work, were fled every one to his field." Why did they do that? They left and got jobs out in the fields. Why? Because nobody was tithing. Nobody was giving. They couldn't just work in the temple all day because their family's needs were not met, and they didn't have food to eat. Nehemiah straightened them out in verse 11. "Then contended I with the rulers, and said, **<u>Why is the house of God forsaken</u>?** And I gathered them together, and set them in their place." Today we'd say, "He set them straight." Do you think Nehemiah set them straight? He's the governor and has a lot of power and control there.

Verse 12 says, "Then brought all Judah the tithe of the corn and the new wine and the oil unto the treasuries." Do you believe after that there was plenty?

What if everybody tithed? There's a scripture passage that shows what happens when everybody tithes. It's called "heaps of heaps."

Second Chronicles 31:4-10:
"Moreover he commanded the people that dwelt in Jerusalem to give the portion of the priests and the Levites, that they might be encouraged in the law of the LORD. And as soon as the commandment came abroad, the children of Israel brought in abundance the firstfruits of corn, wine, and oil, and honey, and of all the increase of the fields; and the tithe of all things brought they in abundantly. And concerning the children of Israel and Judah, that dwelt in the cities of Judah, they also brought in the tithe of oxen and sheep, and the tithe of holy things which were consecrated unto the LORD

*their God, and laid them by **heaps**. In the third month they began to lay the foundation of the **heaps**, and finished them in the seventh month. And when Hezekiah and the princes came and saw the **heaps**, they blessed the LORD, and his people Israel. Then Hezekiah questioned with the priests and the Levites concerning the **heaps**. And Azariah the chief priest of the house of Zadok answered him, and said, Since the people began to bring the offerings into the house of the LORD, we have had enough to eat, and have left plenty: for the LORD hath blessed his people; and that which is left is this great store."*

This is a wonderful picture of what happens when God's people actually tithe and give offerings. The provision was so abundant they had "heaps" left over!

But as you know, this is definitely not the situation in many churches and ministries.

Honor and Blessing

How many people do you think are *not* blessed like they should be in the church? They perpetually don't have enough. And the enemy is devouring their things, and it shouldn't be happening. They're having problem after problem after problem, and loss after loss after loss. They get ahead one step and get knocked back two. How much is that happening in the church all over? Is that the result of being blessed?

Next we will look at 1 Corinthians 9:1 in the Complete Jewish Bible. Is 1 Corinthians 9 in the New Testament? The Holy Spirit is talking through Paul. Does this apply to us? Are we part of the same New Testament church? Let's be clear on this.

Paul said, "Am I not a free man? Am I not an emissary," that's the word for "apostle," "…of the Messiah? Haven't I seen Yeshua our Lord?" Did you know that Paul saw Him more than once? "And aren't you yourselves the result of my work for the Lord?" This church of Corinth didn't exist until the Lord sent Paul there. "Even if to others I am not an [apostle], at least I am to you; for you are living proof that I am the Lord's emissary [apostle]." (vv. 1-2)

The Lord sent him to Corinth, and now they have a church. Is that important? Is that significant? The Lord could have used somebody else. On one occasion He told them, "For though ye have ten thousand instructors in Christ, yet have ye not many fathers: for in Christ Jesus I have begotten you through the gospel. Wherefore I beseech you, be ye followers of me." (1 Corinthians 4:15-16)

Should we respect our elders and our fathers in the faith? Continue reading verse 3. "That is my defense when people put me under examination. Don't we have the right to be given food and drink? Don't we have the right to take along with us a believing wife, as do the other emissaries," or apostles, "also the Lord's brothers and Kefa?" (vv. 3-5) That's Peter. He's talking

Honor and Blessing

about being supported, including his family—being supported financially and materially. Isn't that what he's talking about? Read the whole eighth and ninth chapters. They are some of the richest in the New Testament on this subject.

"Or are Bar-Nabba [Barnabas] and I the only ones required to go on working for our living?" (v. 6) Are they the only ones that have to work, talking about side jobs, natural jobs, for their living? "Did you ever hear of a soldier paying his own expenses?" (v. 7) They give him an assignment: go over here, do this mission, and he says, "Well, as soon as I can get gas for the Humvee. As soon as we can get the money together and buy some ammunition." No. No. All the expenses are paid. "Or of a farmer planting a vineyard without eating its grapes? Who shepherds a flock without drinking some of the milk? What I am saying is not based merely on human authority, because the *Torah*," the Law, "says the same thing." (v. 8) Is this the New

Testament? Is he quoting the Law? Why would he quote the Law? Because the precedent applies to us. The truth applies to us. If it didn't, he wouldn't refer to it.

Are many people trying to tell us that most everything in the Old Testament is not applicable to us anymore? It's all old, and it's all passed away. Is that true or not? Then why would you refer to it like this in the New Testament?

Continue reading verse 8. "What I am saying is not based merely on human authority, because the Torah says the same thing." We've already talked about this. You have two sources of what you believe: human authority—what people have decided with no scriptures for it, and what God has said, that will never change.

"For in the *Torah* (Law) of Moshe (Moses) it is written, 'You are not to put a muzzle on an ox when it is treading out the grain.'" Is that Old Testament? Why is he talking about it in the New? He said, "If God is concerned about cattle, all the more does he say this for our sakes." (v. 9) He was just talking about Barnabas and himself and other preachers having a right to be sustained and supplied. "Yes, it was written for us, meaning that he who plows and he who threshes should work expecting to get a share of the crop. If we have sown spiritual seed among you, is it too much if we reap a material harvest from you?" (vv. 10-11) Is that a principal that whoever sows to you spiritually, you should sow to them materially? Is that a principal in the Word of God? It is. "If others are sharing in this right to be supported by you, don't we have a greater claim to it?" He's the one who started the church there. "But we don't make use of this right. Rather, we put up with all kinds of things so as not to impede in any way the Good News about the Messiah."

And I feel exactly that same way, personally. Though we have a right to be supported through those we minister to, it's not faith or love to demand or require it of them. If it's not done willingly, it's unacceptable.

"Don't you know that those who work in the Temple get their food from the Temple?" (vv. 12-13) Isn't that what we were just reading about? Does what we were reading about in Deuteronomy, Leviticus, and Nehemiah have any application for us today? When the New Testament quotes it, refers to it, and says it applies to us, then it does.

"Don't you know that those who work in the Temple get their food from the Temple, and those who serve at the altar get a share of the sacrifices offered there? **In the same way**, the Lord directed that those who proclaim the Good News should get their living from the Good News." (vv. 13-14) Did you see these words? ***"IN THE SAME WAY..."*** The Spirit of God through Paul is saying that it is God's will and plan for His

New Covenant ministers to be provided for **IN THE SAME WAY** his ministers were provided for in the Old Covenant.

Let me give you some other scriptures in the New Testament. I want to be thorough.

First Timothy 5:17-18. "Let the elders that rule well be counted worthy of double honour, especially they who labour in the word and doctrine. **For the scripture saith**, thou shalt not muzzle the ox that treadeth out the corn. And, The labourer is worthy of his reward." He keeps referring to that. First Thessalonians 5:12-13. "…know them which labour among you, and are over you in the Lord, and admonish you; And to esteem them very highly in love for their work's sake. And be at peace among yourselves."

Romans 15:27. "For if the Gentiles have been made partakers of their spiritual things, their duty is also to minister unto them in carnal things." Do we have a duty?

Galatians 6:6 (Amplified Bible, Classic Edition). "Let him who receives instruction in the Word [of God] share all good things with his teacher [contributing to his support]."

Galatians 6:6 (Living Bible). "Those who are taught the Word of God should help their teachers by paying them."

In Matthew 10 and also in Luke 10, Jesus quoted that "the laborer is worthy of his hire."
Do you think we've established in Scripture that this principle is true and right, and it's true and right for us now, in the New Covenant?

Years ago, I was up north in a meeting, and while I was praying about the service, the Lord brought a pastor to my mind and said to me—not an audible voice, but inside me—that He was displeased with this pastor's car. That it was inadequate, and He wasn't satisfied with it. I thought, *Wow!* I had no idea what kind of car he had or didn't have. And the Lord communed with me further, *When you get home, you get in that little airplane that I just gave you…* (We had just taken delivery of a little single-engine airplane, the first one we ever had.) *And you fly over there. Don't announce yourself, just fly over there…* I don't mean I heard a voice, but this was coming from my spirit to my mind. *And when you get there, he's going to find out you're there, and he's going to contact you. He's going to ask you to speak at their church, and I want you to. And when you do, this is what you preach on:* **God Gave Gifts to Men**.

What do you reckon happened? I flew over there, and in about six hours, the phone rang where I was staying, and the pastor said, "Hey, I didn't know you were in town."

And I said, "Yeah, just got here."

He said, "Are you going to be here over Sunday?"

I said, "Yeah."

He said, "Come speak for me."

I said, "You want me to?" You have to play it cool, you know.

And he said, "Yeah, yeah, please.

I said, "Okay, sure, we'll be there."

And this was what the Lord showed me. I had a watch, a nice watch that an elder of mine in the Gospel had given me. It was expensive. It didn't cost me a dime, but it cost him plenty; he had given it to me to commemorate a goal I had reached in my pilot training. I also had a Timex® watch that was made out of rubber; I swam in it. The Lord brought that to my mind, and He said, "When you come in and you have that dress watch on, you pull it off, you wipe the perspiration off of it, and you have a box that you put it in, and you close the box. Then you set that box in a place where it won't get knocked off and damaged. When you come in from swimming and you have that rubber Timex on, you pull it off and throw it in the corner. It may bounce off the counter and hit the floor, and you don't care. You may let it lay there for days."

Why do we treat one so differently from the other? One I value highly, and the other, I *don't* value highly. Didn't he say, "Esteem them very highly in love for their work's sake." That's talking about a valuation; that's talking about honor.

The Lord showed me this concerning that pastor. I didn't know what kind of car he had, but I found out later it had a lot of miles on it and was worn out. It should have been replaced a long time ago. And the Lord dealt with me and said, "The people at that church don't value the pastors I have given them as they should. What they don't realize is those ministers are My gifts to them. And I can send them somewhere else tomorrow. And if they don't begin to value them more, some things are going to change. And you tell them, you preach on this, Ephesians, you preach on "God gave gifts to men." You talk about this some, and then you bring up what I told you, and then you have your offering ready, and you tell them that if they don't get him a new car, you are."

I thought, *Whoa, I am? I am?* And it's not like we had a whole lot of money back then. I said, "Yes, Sir. Whatever You say."

I didn't come across hard with them, but it was serious. You could tell that. So I did. I preached on it, and I told them what the Lord told me—that He wasn't happy with their pastor's car and that situation. Do you understand that this is about a lot more than a car? The car is a symptom of the problem. I told them that the Lord wanted their pastor to have a new vehicle, and if they wanted to get involved, it would be good, and if they didn't, that we would take care of it.

Oh, man. The Spirit of God moved in that place. People jumped up, they hollered, they gave. And in just a few days, they ordered him a top-notch vehicle with a bunch of extra stuff on it. And they paid for it. Then a year or two after that, they got the pastor and his family a house. That same day, after I preached and the people responded like they did, the Word of the Lord came to me, and I prophesied to them and said, "The next time I'm here, there will be a lot of new cars in this parking lot." And there were. A year or so later, I was there, and there were numerous new cars in the parking lot.

Is there a connection between the ministry and the people? Is our prosperity linked together? Are we connected? Yes, but it involves the tithe and the honor and the blessing.

One of the things we have to understand is that the blessing is not just "well wishing." In Western culture, the blessing has been reduced to wishing someone well. What many people know about "blessing" is when somebody sneezes. They say, "Bless you." The reason they say that is because they think the same thing about any other application of blessing. What do they believe is happening when they say, "God bless you?" Probably nothing. It's just wishing them well, which is insulting in light of what the Word says about the holy powerful Blessing of the Almighty God.

Say this out loud: **The power of the blessing is in the multiplication of the seed.**

It would do us good to say that another hundred times!

When you bring your offering, what do you want to happen? You want a miracle. You want one to turn into ten, or twenty, or fifty, or a hundred. You want a miracle. We live in a world where this is all around us. When you plant a seed, and one seed turns into fifty, that's a miracle. This is why we have food to eat every day.

There used to be two human beings on this planet. Now there are over seven billion. *Billion.* Do you know why? It's because God blessed them and said, **"<u>Be fruitful and multiply</u>."**

Is He just "wishing us well"? Was He saying, *Sure hope y'all do good. Hope it turns out good for you...* That's what the blessing has been reduced to among many Christians.

But in the Old Testament, and into the New Testament, during the early days of the Church, people reverenced and valued the blessing. They hungered for it. They wanted the elders of God to bless them. They wanted the prophet to bless them. It says that they brought little children to Jesus,

Honor and Blessing

didn't they? What did they want Him to do? Bless them.

One of the clearest examples of the power of the blessing is the multiplication of the loaves and fishes. The Bible says the Lord held up the little boy's lunch and gave thanks for it and blessed it. The next thing we see, five loaves and two fishes have turned into everybody being fed with baskets left over. Is that a miracle? What caused that miracle? The power of the blessing.

Here's what you need to know: a million times zero is zero. Bless what? Multiply what? A vague desire? A broad, vague religious notion? No. They brought their tithes. They brought their offerings. They brought something tangible. This represents their life. This is their time. This is their labor and their effort. You don't bless *nothing*; you bless *something*. In order for it to be multiplied, it has to be something. *Be fruitful and multiply* releases miracle-working power.

Say this out loud: **God said, Be fruitful and multiply. Be fruitful and multiply.**

The word *fruitful* literally means "to bear fruit." It means "to produce." So we're talking about the enablement and anointing of God on your life to produce something, not to be barren and produce nothing. Would you like to produce something every day on the job, and in your family? What do you need to produce something worthwhile? You need the blessing—and also "to multiply," which means "to increase, to become numerous, to become great."

Have you ever read it? "Be fruitful and multiply." He said it in Genesis. He said it over the creation of the world that He made. He said it to Abraham. He said it to Noah. He said it to David. He said it over and over and over. Why? Because it is the power of the blessing that causes the seed sown to become fruitful and multiply, the one becoming many.

Ezekiel 44:28 says, "And it shall be unto them for an inheritance: I am their inheritance: and ye shall give them no possession in Israel: I am their possession." He's talking about the Levites and the priest. "They shall eat the meat offering, and the sin offering, and the trespass offering: and every dedicated thing in Israel shall be theirs." (v. 29) I'm telling you, they had a lot of provision, a *lot* of income. "And the first of all the firstfruits of all things, and every oblation of all, of every sort of your oblations, shall be the priest's: ye shall also give unto the priest the first of your dough, that he may cause," what? Why? You give the priest the first of your dough, why? **That *he* may cause "the blessing to rest in thine house.**" (v. 30)

Some people believe that no man or woman down here has any power to bless—that only God can bless. But the truth is, He blesses through people, too, and He does it by the anointing, by the call.

Hebrews 11:20 talks about this. "By faith Isaac blessed Jacob and Esau concerning things to come." Who blessed them? Isaac blessed them. "By faith Jacob, when he was a dying, blessed both the sons of Joseph; and worshipped…." (v. 21) Who blessed them? Jacob did. The Bible talks about David blessing his house. There are numerous places where you see people blessing other people. And yet, the Bible says, "The less is blessed of the greater." (Hebrews 7:7) Now that doesn't mean somebody is a better person than you, or that God loves them more, or that they are more important to God. It's talking about a greater call, a greater anointing. We should always defer and show respect to the higher anointing. Also, you shouldn't be open to just anybody who runs up and says, "I'm going to bless you." Who are they? What relationship are they to you? How do they have any greater place of anointing to bless you?

The same anointing that qualifies for leadership—if someone is anointed to shepherd or to lead or to oversee—is the same anointing that would enable them to bless you. It's not by human effort or power, but by the anointing of His Spirit.

Note these specific instructions from the Holy Spirit to multiple churches in the New Testament…

"Now concerning the collection for the saints, as I have given order to the churches of Galatia, even so do ye. Upon the first day of the week let every one of you lay by him in store, as God hath prospered him, that there be no gatherings when I come." (1 Corinthians 16:1-2)

Several other translations say, "…lay by him at home."

One of the big reasons people don't give is because they don't have it. But they don't have it because they never made the commitment to give to God what is God's.

This is not about tithing to a church. Tithe to the Lord. Give to Him what is His. Separate what's His from yours. Take ten percent off of all your increase, and then add an offering in there, even if it's just one percent, and separate it from *yours*. Put it in in your God Account. If you'll do that every time you make money and get increase, it will accumulate. Whose money is that? It's not yours. You don't pay your bills with it, and you don't buy yourself something you want with it. You don't buy things for your kids. It's not your money. It's God's money for God's things.

We saw precedent in the scripture that the tithe was to go so "that there may be meat [and provision] in mine house" and for the ministers and for those in need. (Malachi 3:10) So as the Lord leads you and directs you, you take of your tithes and your offerings, and you put them into His churches and ministries and to the poor of His people that are hurting and in need.

My wife and I and our churches and ministries have been practicing this for years, and our giving is now at a level we wouldn't have imagined years ago.

Truly God is faithful to His Word. If we honor Him, He will honor us. If we provide for His things, He will pour out blessing and abundance on us and rebuke the devourer for our sakes.

The blessing of the Lord, it makes rich, and He adds no sorrow with it.

If you are convinced of these Bible truths, gather any who are joined to you in family or ministry or business, and without delay, make the commitment to honor the Lord in the tithe, which is His.

Honor and Blessing

You can say this together if it is in your heart(s):

Great God and Father,
I worship You.
You are my God, my Source, and Supply.
Without You, I would be and would have nothing.
But I'm not without You.
I'm am Yours, and You are Mine.
Your banner over me is love.
As you enable me and prosper me,
I commit to put You first and to honor You with the tithe and with offerings.
As I do, I thank You for rebuking the devourer for my sake and for pouring out blessing on us until it overflows.
Get glory to Yourself in us in every area and every way.
We will give You all the glory. Amen.

CONFESSION OF TITHING

Deuteronomy 26; Proverbs 3:9; Isaiah 48:17; Psalm 1:3; Deuteronomy 28: 8

Lord Jesus my High Priest, My Lord and my God, I bring to You my tithes and offerings.
I honor You with my substance and with the firstfruits of all my increase.
Every good thing I have is from Your hand, and I give now willingly and gladly.
I give You thanks and worship You. I rejoice in every good thing You've given me.

(pause and praise and worship)

I was lost and in bondage, but You have saved me.
You've healed me, You've delivered me, and You've made me rich.
You are my Protector and my Provider, my Source and Abundant Supply.
You've made us the head and not the tail.

We'll always be on top, never on the bottom.
I thank You and I worship You for raising me up.

(pause and praise and worship)

You are leading me in the right way and teaching me to prosper.
Everything I put my hand to prospers.
I always have more than enough. I eat the good of the land.
I am blessed of my God, Creator of the heavens and earth.
Make me a blessing to many.

TITHING ADDENDUM TO A MARRIAGE CEREMONY

Many of the couples who we've married in our churches have chosen to include a commitment to tithe in their marriage vows. The following is an example:

_____ and _____ want to acknowledge this day before all, that the Lord their God is, and will always be, the Source and Provider for their house.

As a part of their covenant with each other and the Lord, they commit to Him this day, that they will honor God and put Him first as He prospers them.

(Repeat after me…)

- **The Lord is our Source and Provider.**
- **We will honor the Lord with our substance and with the firstfruits of all our increase.**

- **We will bring to Him the tithe and offerings.**
- **The Lord is our Good Shepherd; we shall not want.**

Lord, by the anointing on me as your minister, I speak blessing over them…

- **The Lord increase you more and more, you and all your household.**
- **Be blessed and prosper and enjoy abundance.**

The Blessing of the Lord, It Maketh Rich, and He Adds No Sorrow With It.

Works Cited: Bibles

Amplified Bible, Classic Edition. Copyright © 1954, 1958, 1962, 1964, 1965, 1987 by The Lockman Foundation.

Complete Jewish Bible. Copyright © 1998 by David H. Stern. All Rights Reserved.

Good News Translation, Copyright © 1992 by American Bible Society.

Holy Bible, New International Version®. NIV®. Copyright © 1973, 1978, 1984 by International Bible Society. Used by permission of Zondervan. All rights reserved.

King James Version, public domain. All Scripture quotations, unless otherwise indicated, are taken from the King James Version of the Bible.

The Living Bible. Copyright © 1971. Used by permission of Tyndale House

Publishers, Inc., Wheaton, IL 60189. All rights reserved.

THE MESSAGE, Copyright © 1993, 2002, 2018 by Eugene H. Peterson. Used by permission of NavPress. All rights reserved. Represented by Tyndale House Publishers, Inc.